What a President Should Know

(But Most Learn Too Late)

WHAT A PRESIDENT SHOULD KNOW

(But Most Learn Too Late)

AN INSIDER'S VIEW ON HOW TO SUCCEED IN THE OVAL OFFICE

LAWRENCE B. LINDSEY

WITH MARC SUMERLIN

ROWMAN & LITTLEFIELD PUBLISHERS, INC.

Lanham · Boulder · New York · Toronto · Plymouth, UK

ROWMAN & LITTLEFIELD PUBLISHERS, INC.

Published in the United States of America
by Rowman & Littlefield Publishers, Inc.
A wholly owned subsidiary of The Rowman & Littlefield Publishing Group, Inc.
4501 Forbes Boulevard, Suite 200, Lanham, Maryland 20706
www.rowmanlittlefield.com

Estover Road
Plymouth PL6 7PY
United Kingdom

Distributed by National Book Network

British Library Cataloguing in Publication Information Available

Library of Congress Cataloging-in-Publication Data

Lindsey, Lawrence.
    What a president should know— but most learn too late : an insider's view on how to succeed in the Oval Office / Lawrence B. Lindsey with Marc Sumerlin.
        p. cm.
    Includes bibliographical references and index.
    ISBN-13: 978-0-7425-6222-6 (cloth : alk. paper)
    ISBN-10: 0-7425-6222-0 (cloth : alk. paper)
    1. Presidents—United States. 2. United States—Politics and government—2001–
3. Presidents—United States—Staff. 4. Lindsey, Lawrence. I. Sumerlin, Marc, 1970–
II. Title.
JK516.L45 2008
352.23'8—dc22   2007025238

Printed in the United States of America

⊚™ The paper used in this publication meets the minimum requirements of Ameri-can National Standard for Information Sciences—Permanence of Paper for Printed Library Materials, ANSI/NISO Z39.48-1992.

To Those Who by Their Sacrifice
Remind Us That Freedom Is Not Free

A president's hardest task is not to do what is right, but to know what is right. Yet the presidency brings no special gift of prophecy or foresight. You take an oath, you step into an office, and you must then help guide a great democracy.

PRESIDENT LYNDON BAINES JOHNSON, January 4, 1965

CONTENTS

INSIDE THE OVAL, AGAIN

THE LORD gave me at least my fair share of character flaws, but a taste for larceny wasn't one of them. Nor was extreme risk taking. So, breaking into the Oval Office, one of the most tightly guarded rooms on the planet, was not a natural thing for me to want to do.

Granted, I wasn't going to take anything. My goal was just to leave something behind. So, if I was caught, theft was not what I was going to be charged with. Nor was the charge going to be breaking and entering. I've been there many times, and it isn't like there was some lock that I was going to jimmy or window that I was going to smash. Still, unless I was very clever, I was quite confident that the government would find something to charge me with.

A knowledge of the inner workings helped. I would need at least two coconspirators; one of them would be the next president of the United States. Actually, all I would need from him would be his silence. The papers that I was going to leave for him were intended for his eyes only, and he really didn't have anything to gain from sharing them. My other conspirator would have to be a member of the outgoing administration—easier to arrange perhaps, but it would involve imposing on a long friendship.

The most ticklish problem was the timing. Any paper that the president of the United States got after he was president would be turned over to the National Archives for display in the Presidential Library. The putative reason for this was to preserve for future historians the thinking that went into presidential decisions.

Like so much else in government, it was full of unintended consequences. The most obvious was that it stifled candor, at least in writing. Who would want to be as blunt with the president in a memo when the ultimate readership wasn't just him but every literate person on the planet? So, the papers had to get to the president before noon on January 20, 2009.

But until then, the president-elect would have his own retinue of retainers and soon-to-be officeholders around. There were only a few moments when the president-elect was alone in the Oval. By custom, that happened on Inauguration Day. The president-elect would go to the White House. The departing incumbent would greet him. They and their spouses would have coffee, and then the president and president-elect would stroll over together to the West Wing, and the president would show his successor his new office.

Here it would get particularly tricky. Some knowledge of George W. Bush would certainly help. First, he was an early riser. My suspicion was that he would be up bright and early, showered and dressed, and over to the Oval for one last look at the place by himself. The staff, if they were around at all, would be preoccupied with emptying their offices, as they had to be out of them by noon. Second, Bush was a real gentleman, with a particular sense of propriety about making sure he did whatever it took to ease the transition for his successor.

Letting his successor have a moment alone in the Oval to contemplate what lies ahead would certainly strike Bush as the right thing to do. Bush would likely walk over with his successor along the covered walkway by the Rose Garden. Even though it was cold, they would probably make the left turn up the walk leading to the Rose Garden entrance to the Oval rather than using the interior entrance. There, at the double doors of paneled glass, Bush would open the door and say something like, "It's all yours. Good luck." He would then shake hands and walk back to the residence to join their spouses in small talk. The president-elect would have a few minutes alone in the Oval before he too would return to the residence. Or at least that was what I was counting on.

If everything played out as planned, the president-elect would find my package under the courtesy note that the departing president would leave on the desk. Far be it from me to try to leave the impression that the package was from the president. The president-elect had better get used to having papers stacked up before him, each from a different person on a variety of topics. But my plan didn't require that the president-elect think that the courtesy note was attached to the package. His curiosity would doubtless be aroused, if not by the package itself, then by the discrete label in the upper-right corner bearing the words "To Be Read in Private When the Need Arises."

Okay, I'll admit that might be a bit dramatic. But I wasn't going to take any chances once the plan got that far. He would open the package and see an actual briefing book: a standard one-inch three-ring binder with a set of memos inside. The notebook would be quite similar to what he would have to take back to the residence each night, except for the cover label. This would doubtless cause him to at least glance at what lay below and note the package of memos. Pressed for time, he would realize that now was not the moment. He would try to figure out what to do with the papers and realize that this was now his office and that this was now his desk. He would open the top right-hand drawer and deposit the papers inside. They would be there, just like the cover said, "To Be Read in Private When the Need Arises."

That would be followed by a glance at the watch, a deep sigh, and a final look around the room. Today was a day for ceremony, the oldest celebration of the peaceful and democratic transition of power on the planet. Work was for tomorrow.

It was a great vision, anyway. The key, as with most things, was the timing. The memo had to be put in place between the outgoing president's last visit and his return with his soon-to-be successor. Sometime between 8:00 and 9:00 in the morning seemed ideal, but the actual timing would require being pre-positioned and ready to grab opportunity when it presented itself.

This meant bringing my other coconspirator, the outgoing economic policy adviser, into the loop. We had both served in two administrations, so I knew that after the initial shock, he would find the idea intriguing.

He took the call himself and agreed to my request for a rendezvous early in his office on Inauguration Day. I knew he would be there on his last day. There is something distinctly pleasurable about watching the heavy metal gates of the compound swing open as you drive in for the last time. And on that last day, you get to notice how your chest puffs out an inch or two as you walk in the basement entrance, steps away from your parking place, while a Secret Serviceman welcomes your arrival. All those other days you are too busy to smell the proverbial roses. The greatest thing about your last day is that you can fully savor the trappings on the way in, knowing when you leave that someone else will be shouldering the responsibility.

Yes, he would be there. He would want to savor the moment but, unlike the incoming president, not necessarily alone. He was not by nature a solitary man. Besides, we were the bookends of national economic policy for this president's two terms.

Of course, I didn't fill him in on the details over the phone. I just promised to bring the champagne, orange juice, and glasses for some early morning mimosas. Besides, the phones were tapped on a routine basis, and having the Secret Service find out about the plan in advance just wouldn't work.

I was even cleared in to park on West Executive Avenue at 7:30 A.M., a real honor for someone on the outside. Maybe he actually preferred to have company and the chance to reminisce. Maybe it was the mimosas that sealed the deal. It was then that I felt some momentary guilt. I was using him and candidly wouldn't blame him if he just called the guard. But I had a hunch he wouldn't.

In fact, the reprimand I got when I sat down at his conference table and explained my real purpose was fairly mild. "Meddling again LL?" was all he said. Meddling, especially in public policy, when prudence would dictate otherwise, was one of those character flaws I had in abundance. We both knew it.

He took the bottle of Clos du Mesnil from the table and refilled the glasses. Champagne is meant for sipping, not swigging, but this was one of those swigging moments. Jack Daniels would have been more appropriate.

He was someone who it would have been fun to have had as a fraternity brother in college. In fact, this caper was just up his alley. No real harm done. Just enough risk to get the adrenaline pumping. Besides, it would be a great story to tell our grandkids. And at our age, grandkids were a lot closer in time than were our college days.

When I handed him the package, he looked at the envelope and joked, "Hey, where's the red dot? I thought you said this was important." It was part of his ironic sense of humor and was delivered in his accent that smacked of his southern upbringing. It also brought back memories of our first days working together. The stick-on red dots, each a bit less than an inch in diameter, indicated a need for immediate attention. Of course, every sender thinks that the package he is sending needs immediate attention, so most such envelopes carry red dots. Nearly two decades earlier, this had led some unthinking staff assistants to begin attaching two or three red dots to each envelope, leading to what became known as "red dot inflation."

"It is important. We could have used something like this eight years ago. Even though the president watched what his dad went through, it still wasn't the same as having it happen to him personally. The job wears down even the best man over eight years, and we both know he's a darn good one. You've known him for more than thirty years. How much of the man you once knew is still there?"

It was a rhetorical question but still one that needed to be repeated because it refocused us on the big picture. He had been ground down for the past four years by the need to get through each day without another crisis. It was easy to lose sight of the big picture. I had been out for six years. It had been time enough for me to recharge and time enough for me to care again. It didn't matter who was entering the office just below us; the new president deserved to know what he was about to get hit with. And the country needed him to be prepared.

We stood up together and walked down the narrow back staircase that leads from the second floor down to the main level where the Oval Office sits. The real West Wing is not like its television namesake. The corridors are much narrower, and the stairs usually require that someone coming down pause on the side to let the person climbing pass by. On the main level, it was a right out of the stairwell and then a left down the corridor.

A smile crossed my face as we turned the corner. The duty guard outside the Oval was Mike, who recognized me instantly. Seven years earlier, he had called out a "thanks" to me from one of the guard booths. I had responded with an instinctive "You're welcome," followed by a "for what?" He had just gotten his first paycheck for 2002 and had already done the math. "The tax cut will mean a bit more than 2,000 bucks for us this year." I had said, "Thank the president, don't thank me."

I was glad it was meaningful in a tangible way to someone real. I had spent most of my time on the big picture, making sure it helped to minimize a recession. That happens a lot in Washington. The "macroeconomy" we all focus on is really just a large collection of people like Mike and his family. It was really thoughtful of him that every time he had seen me since, he had mentioned it, including again today.

I asked about his two boys and was informed that th
was going to graduate in June. Tip O'Neill was wrong. All politics
isn't local; it's personal. I guess that is just the political analogue to
macroeconomics.

My coconspirator asked, "Mind if we take a last look?"

"Well sir, your pass will get you in, but not Mr. Lindsey. Sorry,
sir, those are the rules."

We actually knew that, and I was counting on it. "I'll just stand
here and chat for a while; you go ahead." I positioned myself to
look in, which, of course, also forced Mike to look out. We continued our chat about family and work, and I managed to discover
that, yes, the president had been here alone, bright and early, and
then gone back to the residence.

In the end, it all seemed too easy. Maybe fate was shining on
me; maybe it was, as I thought, that the rhythms of government
tend to be fairly predictable. But I felt a huge sigh of relief. The
deed was done. I had done all I could do.

What follows is what I left.

FROM: LAWRENCE B. LINDSEY
SUBJECT: GETTING STARTED
January 20, 2009

Congratulations. You've made it.

You must be exhausted. You've been running for this job for at least two years, putting in twelve and fourteen hour days at a minimum and logging close to a million air miles. You've had those cameras and microphones in your face constantly and had every detail of your life scrutinized thoroughly.

Nobody who goes through that ordeal can possibly be the same person he or she was when at the start of the campaign. I've served in the White House under three presidents and been in a senior government position during a fourth. I've seen what running for president and, more important, *being* president does. No one who has been through this remains unaffected.

Notice how everyone has started calling you Mr. President, even people you've known all your life and who have called you by your first name the whole time. Right now they mean it as a form of congratulations, an acknowledgment of your success. But it's not going to stay that way. You are now and forever more the president of the United States. By calling you that, they are reminding both you and themselves that you are the boss and more powerful than any other person on the planet. From now on, every one of them now needs something from you, even if it is only to take their side in some dispute. Over time, it will become less obvious what you need from them. Try as you might, you no longer have any equals.

So now is the best time to recognize what you are going to need from these people, especially your longtime and closest friends. It is honesty. More specifically, it is honesty when you are in the process of making a mistake. Honesty is easy when you're doing great. "Gee, that was a great speech, Mr. President." "You really scored a home run on that one, Mr. President." Sometimes it is simply, "Yes, Mr. President." Trouble is, everyone around you is going to start saying those same things whether or not it was a great speech and whether you actually did hit a home run or, in reality, struck out. By the way, when your wife calls you Mr. President, you better take notice because it is a sound verbal slap that you are really getting too big for your britches.

There is no time like the present to start reinforcing the people who bring you the bad news and not just those who bring you the good. I know this goes against your grain; it would go against anyone's who has an ego. And anyone who runs for president is most assuredly not lacking in that department. Moreover, the exhilaration of being treated like a rock star by cheering crowds and having 60 million people vote for you isn't likely to have increased your modesty.

You are now the boss. Think about it from the perspective of the person working for you. Telling someone's boss something he doesn't want to hear isn't easy in the best of circumstances. Shooting straight with the tough news face-to-face with the most powerful man in the world is even harder.

Moreover, take a look around at your digs. The Oval Office is designed to intimidate, subtly perhaps, but intimidate nonetheless. Who else do you know whose office is oval? It is one of the least efficient uses of space one can imagine. And that door that leads to the corridor outside the Roosevelt Room is actually a cut out of the wall, oval shaped on the inside but not on the outside. It is absolutely soundproof. Then there's the desk. It is made out of the wood of a British Arctic exploration ship that the Americans rescued from the ice and returned to Queen Victoria. When the ship was retired, she had the desk made from its timbers and presented it to President Rutherford B. Hayes on the centennial anniversary of us beating them in our War for Independence. Talk about being the alpha male.

So, the person telling you the bad news to your face in the Oval Office is a rare breed to be cherished and cultivated. You won't think so at the time, but he or she is also doing you a huge favor. It's not like you're not going to be able to hide from the bad news for the next four years. Think of it as a choice. You can have someone tell you the bad news privately in your office while you still have a chance to rescue the situation. Or you can have the bad news splashed across the headlines of every newspaper in the country and be questioned about it constantly by those obnoxious reporters when you are trying to talk about something else.

Today marks one of the toughest adjustments you'll ever have to make—moving from candidate mode to governing mode. You are no longer *applying for the job* with the people of the United States. You have it. You are now chief executive officer of the most powerful nation in the history of the world. Everyone wants a decision from you. They will want you to make more decisions than you ever thought possible. Many of those decisions will be about things you haven't even thought about or read about. How will you get the information you need to make the right call? How will you know what options are available to you? How will you make sure that your decision has been implemented? What decisions will you delegate? How will you be sure that the people you delegate to actually would do something similar to what you would want to have done?

This briefing book is designed to help you in two ways. First, it will give you some of the unvarnished background about the policy issues you are going to face. When you're confronted by a decision and all the choices seem bad and you're wondering how you ever got into this situation, it is usually not because of the immediate issue at hand but because something more fundamental is broken. *Fundamental problems are tough things to fix, which is why your predecessors left them for you.* You, in turn, will be able to fix some and will have no choice but to leave some for your successors. It also gives you the options on some of the key policy issues you will confront.

The second objective of the briefing book is to tell you *how* to make decisions. That may sound presumptuous to be telling someone who 60 million people just picked to be the nation's key decision maker. But there are things about decision making that you don't know now but will know in four years. Both you and the country might be better off if you figured them out sooner rather than later. Besides, unlike all those people around you calling you "Mr. President," all I can say is "been there, done that."

I wrote these briefs well before I knew who you would turn out to be. (And, if you turned out to be Hillary Clinton, I hope that you will accept my deepest apologies for the use of the male form in these memos. You had as much chance as anyone, and I tried writing "Mr. or Madam President" and "he or she," but stylistically it didn't work. Besides, having spent eight years here already and knowing the challenges, you would probably be the most tolerant of any lapse.)

I also knew that whoever you turned out to be, I wouldn't want anything from you and that there would be only about a 50-50 chance that I even voted for you. Consider me sufficiently disinterested to be able to be honest. But should our paths actually cross sometime I will still call you Mr. President just like everyone else, even if my motives are different. From me it will be a sign of respect for the responsibilities you are carrying and sympathy for what you are about to go through.

THE CORRUPTING WALLS
OF THE WEST WING

MOST PEOPLE have no idea why the West Wing was created. The story is simple enough, one that any family could easily appreciate. Edith Roosevelt was a sensible woman and not without influence. She was tired of the president's advisers hanging around all the time on the second floor of the mansion, the same floor that she and Teddy and their six children lived on.

So work began on constructing a new structure on the west side of the White House, just across the street from the Executive Office Building that housed the War, State, and Navy departments. For the first time, the White House became a home, and the president's advisers had a place they could stay all night long. It may have been a family-friendly move, but it also initiated a more far-reaching change in the executive branch. The insular culture of power in the West Wing was born.

Teddy's new office was as angular as his prickly personality. It wasn't until William Howard Taft assumed office in 1909 that an Oval Office was created. Oval better reflected Taft's body type, which the press mocked. But his mind was sharp, and so were his political instincts and understanding of the need for access to power.

Taft placed the original Oval right in the middle of the West Wing, approximately where the room we now call the Roosevelt Room was located. It was a very clever decision both symbolically and practically. He wanted to be at the center of decision making, and the oval shape allowed multiple advisers to have direct access to him. Their offices surrounded his, and an oval shape maximized the diameter (and therefore the number of offices that could touch his) for a given-size office relative to a rectangle. At the same time, the elongated shape permitted space for both a conference table and a working desk.

Taft liked the shape of his new office for another reason. It matched the oval-shaped Blue Room of the residence. These rooms without corners dated to George Washington, who first had them in his personal residence. Washington, leader of the new Republic, liked the egalitarian aspect of a room with no foot or head. Witnesses would note, however, that he would always be found in the direct center. He was a natural leader of men and couldn't escape this fact, no matter how closely to his breast he held the ideal of equality. For Martha Washington, a curved room created a natural flow for parties and prevented people from getting pushed into the corners. Oval symbolized the republican virtues of the new country. But it also reflected America at the turn of the twentieth century—a nation coming of age.

The physical structure reflected the growing power and involvement of the presidency. Thanks to Teddy Roosevelt, the president was now expected to be involved in all matters of the federal government and to stick his nose into the affairs of private enterprise as well. Of course, we take this for granted now.

In Taft's view, a president sitting at the center, with open access, was in the direct path of information—a beautiful, unfiltered flow of facts, innuendo, and hypotheses. But being surrounded by staff had an unintended consequence. As the power of the presidency grew, so did the power of the West Wing advisers. They formed an outer perimeter around the president that would naturally come to view most information from the outside as competition, treating it as unreliable at best and dangerous at worst. Incoming information needed to be "fact checked," that is, filtered, to protect the president.

More staff with the potential for access also created a need to prioritize who could see the president when. Staff also needed to be informed about what others were telling the president since they also might need to know the same set of facts. This would lead to the creation of ever more sophisticated and complex levels of process to determine who would see what and who would be in what meetings with the president.

Moreover, if the president were to be in a meeting with multiple advisers, each with a different point of view, he might have difficulty separating fact from opinion. The classic presidential line reflecting this was from John F. Kennedy, who in 1963 sent two trusted advisers, Joseph Mendenhall and Major General Victor Krulak, to South Vietnam to tell him what was going on. They came back with completely opposite opinions. Kennedy replied, "You two did visit the same country, didn't you?"

One might think that giving the president a variety of different points of view and letting him make the decision would be a good thing. But not if you are staff. Varied and controversial views make you look bad; having an open argument in front of the president came to be thought of as wasting his time and therefore not serving his interests. The result was that memos to the president had to be precirculated and precleared by all of the key players. This gave everyone a veto. The Oval was well suited to evolve into a bubble. But we are getting a little ahead of our story.

With so much embedded republican virtue, it would take our first king (at least that is what his opponents called him) to expand the place again physically. Franklin Delano Roosevelt, the only president elected four times, renovated the West Wing in 1934 with the express purpose of accommodating more staff.

History might choose to illustrate his pursuit of executive power with his failed 1937 attempt to expand the Supreme Court in order to pack it with his supporters. But his quiet expansion of the Executive Office of the President led to the most lasting increase in the concentration of power at 1600 Pennsylvania Avenue. Not only did he make the West Wing bigger, he moved the Oval Office from the center to a new addition on the southeastern corner. It also allowed more room for staff and for meetings.

The purported reason to move it out of the windowless center was to allow for better light, a brilliant view, easier access from the residence, and a two-story interior. But the result was an Oval Office with a single and more easily controlled point of entry. FDR didn't think of it this way, but in practice the president was now more isolated. The staff was now less supervised. The imperial presidency was on its way.

Parenthetically, FDR also added a bomb shelter during the last year of his presidency and his life. It was placed under a renovated East Wing that houses the First Lady's office. The bomb shelter turned out to be so small that Roosevelt pledged never to return after examining the completed project, even in emergency. "I would rather go to the South Lawn and enjoy the fireworks," he stated. A half century later, I would experience this claustrophobia firsthand, but that is a longer story that I will leave for later.

So, if we now had an Oval Office with an easily defended single entrance, the next natural step was the creation of a palace guard. This next step in the evolution of the West Wing as the center of power was the creation of a chief of staff. It took a military man, Dwight D. Eisenhower, to create such a hierarchical structure. Sherman Adams, the first and longest-serving chief, became the singular point of access to Ike. Rather than have the give-and-take of West Wing Office politics determine who would see the president and what he would read, that power was vested in a single man.

It was doubtless a more efficient way of rationing the president's time. The demands of the job were growing rapidly. But it also meant that the president was one more step removed from reality. The Eisenhower presidency was inseparable from Adams— that is, until the day Adams accepted a Vicuna overcoat from a corrupt businessman. Adams was forced to resign. He wasn't the first person and was by no means the last to be affected by the power and seduction that emanates from the walls of the West Wing. Everyone is susceptible to Potomac Fever, and the longer you stay, the more likely you are to get a severe case.

The Eisenhower model wasn't followed by everyone. President Jimmy Carter had no chief of staff until the end. He was such a micromanager that he kept tabs on the schedule to the White House tennis court. The job of president is too big not to delegate. The key is to determine what to delegate and what not to. Few would believe that the fate of the nation has ever been determined by who got the court next.

It was no surprise that President Ronald Reagan went back to the Adams model. In James Baker, Reagan had a man equal to Adams who allowed Reagan to focus on the most important decisions. Baker was the first chief of staff I ever saw in action, and in many ways he was the model for the job. Simultaneously tough and charming, Baker ran a get-to-the point senior staff meeting in the morning that dictated the progress of events in the White House that day. It also determined how the public would *see* the White House that day. One of the key decisions at the top of the agenda was the "photo-op"—when the president would have his picture taken and in what setting it would take place. Reagan's schedule was the most detailed I have ever seen with timing down to the minute, including scheduled time to move from one event inside the West Wing to another.

It might seem constraining to the president, but Reagan had two key advantages that "let Reagan be Reagan" or, more precisely, that let the Reagan administration be Reagan. First and foremost, Reagan had a philosophy so well formed and well known that delegation was feasible without diluting his agenda. At nearly every staff meeting I attended, the preferences of the president were not in doubt. This made the meetings short. At the most controversial ones—aimed at resolving an ongoing dispute between my boss, Martin Feldstein, and Treasury Secretary Don Regan—the key point in dispute was the *meaning* of the phrase the president used, words the president himself and his speechwriters had settled on to allow ambiguity.

Reagan's second secret was to keep a few key decisions to himself. No bureaucratic process would have allowed a president to utter the words "Evil Empire" or to say something so provocative as "Mr. Gorbachev, tear down this wall." There's a saying in Washington about particularly precocious politicians: "Smart Enough to Be Staff." The staff actually think this way. So, if the politician can show on key occasions that he is "Smarter Than Staff," their control over him is broken.

But if the story so far has been about how the physical development of the West Wing helped the staff isolate the president, the post-Reagan story is also about how the changes in the West Wing have helped isolate the staff. When the West Wing was first built, the road between it and the Executive Office Building was open to traffic—both cars and pedestrians. Long before Reagan, a gate was built blocking off that avenue, known as West Executive Avenue. This allowed the president to move back and forth to the Executive Office Building with a comparative minimum of fuss.

My wife and I worked together for Reagan, and she outranked me as far as perks go. A key one was parking privileges on "State Place," which was just outside the gate. Geographically, the White House complex sits between Pennsylvania Avenue and E Street. Both were open to traffic, and anyone could drive up to the gate right outside the White House simply by bearing right off of E Street.

Tour buses used to go past the White House on E Street and slow to a near crawl as they went by, allowing everyone a chance to take their own picture from the bus. Families would pose along the gate on E Street for a group picture with the South Lawn in the background. During the day, there was a continuous stream of tourists through the first floor of the White House, families from all walks of life and every corner of the country coming to see the president's house—a house that they decided who lived in. As a commuter, I used to curse the buses for the time and frustration they caused. But there was nothing like seeing these families use their nearly unfettered access to their capital city to know that you were working for them and for the greatest experiment in self-government in history.

Then one day, some crazy guy parked a truck outside the Washington Monument and claimed that it was full of explosives. That was the start of our first fear of terrorism. At first, a set of concrete planters was set up outside the gate to West Executive Avenue. With each successive presidency, the security perimeter expanded. Pennsylvania Avenue, E Street, and State Place were closed to traffic under Clinton. Seventeenth Street was closed for part of the Bush presidency. The Executive Office complex now blocks eastbound traffic across Washington for seven full blocks and westbound traffic for eight blocks.

Access to the White House is now far more restricted. The tourists are gone most hours. Those who go through are subject to the same kind of search as airplane passengers. There are no tour buses allowed anywhere close to the building. What used to be a bustling West Wing lobby now typically has but a handful of visitors.

The Oval was turned into a fortified bubble by the staff. Now the staff itself is protected by its own palace guard in what, candidly, is coming to look more and more like a fortress or, perhaps, a bunker. Doubtless this is necessary for security. It is one of those things we call "a fact of modern life" about which we just shrug. But it can't be good for the country.

There is a tragic irony in all this. The power of the presidency has grown enormously since Edith Roosevelt exiled the president's staff to a small building across the Rose Garden. That building, the West Wing, has taken on a life of its own—and even become a symbol of the presidency. But it is an organism that seems to get even stronger when the president himself gets weaker and more isolated. At this point, only a mighty president, with a tremendous force of will and knowledge of what lies ahead, will escape its grasp.

So here is what I warned our next president about his staff.

MEMORANDUM FOR THE PRESIDENT

FROM: LAWRENCE B. LINDSEY
SUBJECT: PERSONNEL IS POLICY
January 20, 2009

At this point you are probably about one-third of the way through hiring the people who are going to staff your administration. You probably have picked your cabinet, most of the deputy secretaries, and most of your senior staff. All told, you will fill about 1,500 slots. These people are your eyes and ears. They are also your megaphones. They will be constantly talking to the rest of Washington directly and indirectly through the press. As chief executive officer, you are responsible for what they say and do.

There was a saying in the Reagan administration that "Personnel Is Policy." Like so many things under Reagan, it never was exactly clear whether the saying originated with Reagan. But it really didn't matter. That was how things were. Everyone hired in that administration knew what direction the president wanted to go and knew that they were there to carry out his wishes. There were always disputes about what *exactly* the president wanted, but there was never a philosophical dispute about what the president believed.

The phrase was most commonly used in Washington to imply an ideological tilt to the staff. Reagan was elected as the quintessential Washington outsider. In fact, the existing Washington establishment considered him dangerous, and in a sense, he was—to them. He brought in like minded people from outside of Washington to implement his agenda. The personnel he hired were meant to implement, and were inseparable from, the policy being implemented. It was often said that these appointees "brought their own agendas with them." Maybe they did, but it was the job of Reagan's Office of Presidential Personnel to hire only those people whose agendas dovetailed with the president's philosophy. They did their job superbly.

Often the pejoratives of ideology and agenda are attached to people who are rigorous but independent thinkers.

Contrast this with another saying about presidential personnel that applied to Reagan's successor, the first President Bush. It was, "We have mortgages, not agendas." It was meant as a contrast with the highly ideological group that Reagan brought in. The Bush hires were highly competent technocrats, not ideologues. Indeed, President Bush ran on and was elected on a program for a "kinder, gentler" America, an implicit nod to the country's desire for less ideology and more pragmatism.

You are also following a president that Washington considers ideological and dangerous. **But don't lose sight of the Reagan lesson: the presidency is about ideas and you need to hire people that share your philosophy**.

UNDERSTANDING MOTIVATION

Understanding the motivations of the people you hire is critical. It will taint what they tell you and will affect how you manage them as individuals. Mr. President, the fact is that most of the people you hire will have both agendas and mortgages, though the emphasis will differ. Regarding mortgages and agendas, there are really three types of people you will hire:

1. **Those with agendas**. These are people, like those who staffed much of the Reagan administration, who are experts in their field and are coming to town to implement their ideas. Your press and political aides will consider them dangerous because in their view they want to use your political capital for their ideas. But these are the natural people to have in top slots because they actually KNOW SOMETHING. It is your job and the job of the Office of Presidential Personnel to make sure their agendas advance your philosophy.

2. **Those with mortgages**. These are part of the permanent government, generally having risen to the senior ranks of the civil service or staff of Capitol Hill. They have made the lifestyle choice of government

service because they like public policy and public service. This is a real asset. Like those with agendas, they also know about the issues you will face because they have seen them before. They are the source of institutional history, and as such they often provide the opposite perspective of those with agendas. While the people coming in from the outside with agendas are trying to make something happen, these people will tend to know why something won't work and know that the devil is always in the details. They are best paired with people with agendas, usually in a deputy role, as their skills naturally complement each other.

3. **Those whose agenda is their mortgage**. They form the back channel of Washington—which you will be oblivious to in your bubble. Typically, these people are affiliated with one of two key parts of the money side of permanent government: lobbying and image consulting. These people will naturally end up in your legislative affairs shops and press departments. Most have great Rolodexes, and you want them on your side. But after they serve the president of the United States, they are going to make eight to ten times what you have paid them working for people who need to get things done in Washington. While they may have the purest of motives on day one, as the weeks and months drag on, as the twelve and fourteen hour days begin to get tiresome, as their spouses complain that the family is being neglected, one by one each of these individuals will think more and more about what they are going to do next. Gradually, their agenda will become their mortgage—and it will be a very big mortgage to be a player on the Washington social circuit. Their mission in life will be to build the relationships that will become permanent in their lives. You are just a temporary boss. Worse, they will come to behave like you need them more than they need you.

PICKING SKILL TYPES

You are looking for four essential skill sets in each of the people you hire. Of course, nobody is perfect. We are all better at some things than others. But you will want to make sure that the people you hire have at least passable skills in each of these basic skill sets and outstanding skills in at least one. As a former professor I like to think of these in grading terms as "an A and three Bs" or "two As, a B and a C."

1. **Persuaders**. At some level politics is all about persuading. To keep your popularity high and to win reelection, you need to persuade the public, primarily through the media, of the wisdom of your policies. To pass legislation, you need to persuade members of Congress to come around to your point of view and accept your approach to solving problems. Popularity is power. Washington has developed a professional persuading class of lobbyists and media specialists. Natural-born persuaders flock to Washington. These people are useful, but they are also the ones most likely to fall into the category above of "their agenda is their mortgage." Persuaders are often lawyers—they are good at arguing one side of a case vigorously while ignoring opposing facts—and find it ethical to do so. This may work in the courtroom but not when the other side is never presented to you.

2. **Thinkers**. Persuasion by itself can be a good thing or a bad thing, depending on the quality of the idea behind the persuasion. The decisions you make will directly or indirectly determine whether thousands of people live or die—whether through war, access to health care, or even in managing a Third World currency crisis. You need quality thinkers. There are always problems to fix *before they become crises*. A brain-dead policy apparatus doesn't know where to look. Worse, it will start to produce policies designed simply to maximize poll numbers. A representative government such as ours adds value over a pure democracy because elected officials exercise judgment and do not simply reflect popular prejudice. An alternative brain-dead approach is simplistically following a doctrinaire set of views without incorporating new information and facts about how things are going. Typically, thinkers have a point of view. They are quintessentially "people with agendas." But in public policy, the thinkers worth hiring also reach out for new information and facts to adjust the course of policy.

3. **Managers**. Woody Allen's saying that "95 percent of life is just showing up" was mostly right. He should have said that "95 percent of a *successful* life is just showing up *prepared.*" That is certainly true of government, where simply making the trains run on time is a good part of the job. You need good managers to organize your administration and your schedule; to organize the flow of your policy proposals; to keep you from violating one of the myriad rules, regulations, and standards that have been set up; and particularly to make sure that there is follow through on the policy proposals you enact. Government tends to be poorly managed in part because the top tiers of the executive branch are viewed by the lifetime civil service employees they manage as "short termers," in for two to four years. You will need to hire exceptional people to make sure that things get done. These will also be the people you rely on in crisis—people who can pull together the full force of the federal government when needed.

4. **Loyalists**. Every administration will end up with its fair share of people who seem to have no particular skill other than a long association with you. Some are true lifelong friends. Some simply made a bet that you were a winner and stuck with you. Loyalty is the most cherished virtue in Washington because everyone is in battle mode and having someone watching your back is vital. But loyalists can also be sycophants. You want people who are loyal to your vision not because you won but because they believe in it too. These are people who are ready to make the sacrifices that come with public service and can also remain straight shooters. A loyalist who can't tell you the truth in private really isn't being loyal at all. If you surround yourself with people who are simply loyal to you for their own sake, the bubble around you will thicken.

The first instinct of your personnel operation is likely to be to hire "the best there is" in each type of skill set. The problem is that will create a "silo" style of organization. Professional persuaders will be brought in to run your congressional relations and media relations operations. Great minds will be brought in from academia and think tanks to create policy. People who have been involved in and helped manage your political career will be brought in to run the whole operation.

Things may go well at first, but in the end this is a recipe for operational disaster. Your professional persuaders will insulate your thinkers from the reality of congressional and public discussion because they will want to do it themselves. By and large, your thinkers are perfectly capable at persuading but probably need help on style, tone, and phrasing. But your persuaders have every incentive to want to do the job themselves. Getting face time with Congressmen and in front of the camera is what helps pay their mortgage in the long run after all. The end result is that thinkers are cut off from the new information that helps them develop the nuances of policy and that most of your persuading is being done by people who don't know firsthand about the issues they are discussing. **Your top advisers must be capable thinkers, managers, and persuaders, and they must be loyal to your vision**.

WHO GETS YOUR EAR

Once you hire your advisers, you have to determine who gets your ear. You'll want to avoid unnecessary buffers, which means holding White House staff to a minimum. The staff of the West Wing will try to "protect you" from the cabinet. But if you neglect your cabinet, they will do their own thing or, more specifically, what the bureaucracy wants. Keep your cabinet members close and they will serve you and not their institution. If you really don't want to see them, it's probably time to replace them. A strong, trusted cabinet will also allow you to focus on the most important issues. If cabinet members are known to have access to you, they will have more authority to solve problems themselves, especially those with Congress.

Even with a strong cabinet, the West Wing will get more powerful over time. There is an inevitable power struggle between title, which the cabinet has, and proximity. Proximity wins. Or, as your predecessor noted to me, "Proximity Is Power." Because the West Wing is so important, it is crucial to get the structure right. The usual White House setup has the policy heads (thinkers and managers) sitting at an equal level with the political, press, and legislative affairs aides (the pure persuaders). In addition to the silo effect mentioned above, there is also the simple fact that the persuaders outnumber and, because of their skill set, outmaneuver the policy team. This breeds conflict, rigged outcomes, and bad decisions.

The legislative affairs staff will come to represent Congress in the White House, not the other way around. The perfectly timed call you receive from the Speaker of the House just before a confidential meeting will not be random. They spend all their time on the Hill and, not being experts in policy, are easily persuaded themselves. They measure their success in deals closed. The more they can persuade you to adopt the Hill position, the more likely they are to get a signing ceremony. You will be sympathetic to them because you want signing ceremonies too. Most will have been lobbyists before—they are hired because they have relationships with members after all—and all will be lobbyists when they leave.

The press aides are concerned about managing the twenty-four-hour news cycle. They want good press for you tomorrow. This is their job, and good press in turn makes their job easier. They will push you to make nonconfrontational decisions. You will be sympathetic to them because you want good press for yourself tomorrow too. They also want good press themselves—it's in their DNA. There is an unguarded secret in town that you are either a source or a target. The most surefire way to get good press is to leak. The most surefire way to get criticized is to be isolated from the press. This is why the press people jealously guard access to the media under the guise of "message control."

The political aides are bloc builders. They want you to court enough organized blocs of voters to build a majority. They are bottom up, poll driven, and vindictive. They have to be because that is the nature of the business. You will be sympathetic to them because they got you here. But their worldview is the opposite of top-down leadership.

The best way to mitigate these power centers is to structure the White House with an emphasis on people who know something about the substance of what it is you are trying to accomplish as opposed to the various processes of getting things done in Washington. Most administrations establish decision-making councils chaired by an assistant to the president with membership that includes the key cabinet officers in that policy sphere. Currently, there are four such councils: the National Security Council, the National Economic Council, the Domestic Policy Council, and the Homeland Security Council. This is where the serious government-wide policy work and interagency coordination happens. This is also how decisions are brought to you. In the next few weeks, you will sign an executive order that sets up the structure of these councils for your administration.

The product of these councils is typically a decision memorandum to you that includes a set of possible options and the recommendations of the members of the council. Typically, it is the job for the assistant to the president who chairs the council to present the decision memo. But this person has the same title and the same rank that a dozen other White House advisers will get. Most of these will be the professional persuaders discussed above who will also demand to be in on the meeting. These assistants are also the natural allies of the chief of staff since his job, like theirs, is primarily process. So when the decision meeting is held in the Oval, sixteen assistants to the president will try to get into the meeting at the exclusion of the cabinet and the experts. As a result, **the vast majority of advisers voicing an opinion to you at the point a final decision is being made will have no knowledge, background, or expertise in the subject**.

They will know how it will play in the press. They will know how particular interest groups will feel about the subject and how key Congressmen will respond. This is important information. But you should at least *start* the process by trying to *do the right thing* and having the inevitabilities of the Washington process move you away from this target. If you start with a political target as opposed to one that fits the realities of the world, you are creating problems for yourself down the road. Think of it this way: if you were going into surgery, would you want the surgeon to be accompanied by the hospital administrator, head of billing, and shop steward for the nurses' union in the operating room?

To mitigate this inevitability, the various experts in process should provide support for your policy councils, not be able to make an end run around them. They could be members of the policy councils, not the equal of the policy councils on matters of policy, when they meet with you. In turn, the heads of those councils and the members of the cabinet should be put in the position of being face-to-face persuaders, a role that the process assistants now play instead. They should meet frequently with members of Congress, the press, and outsiders. Let them feel the political and public pressure that you feel. It will enhance the quality of advice you get and cut down on the amount of back channeling and turf fighting.

There is one other danger: getting bogged down. This is why you need to carefully think about the one buffer that is essential—the chief of staff. When the history books are written, there will be fewer than ten events or policies that define your presidency. Don't get sidetracked on the items that will be of little historic consequence. Everyone will hate this. Your political advisers will want to keep the permanent campaign going, which means giving out goodies to key groups. Your policy advisers will want you to spend your political capital on all their issues—big and small. Your time will be stretched many ways, but you must make sure your schedule reflects your top priorities. The main job of your chief of staff will be to say "no," including to you.

That is why your most important pick in the West Wing will be your chief of staff. A Sherman Adams or a James Baker can be a great asset. The chief of staff must have an instinctive ear for what is crucial and what is superfluous. This means they are good listeners, gathering information from multitudinous sources and quickly determining what you need to hear. They also need to be forward looking, identifying opportunities and problems far enough in advance that you have time to act. They need to be capable of managing the largest organization in the world—the government of the United States. They need to be decisive, tough, and fair. In short, you need to find someone better than you but someone who also has the self-discipline not to end up running things himself. It is virtually impossible to find someone this talented and this humble, but it is your most important hiring decision and one you should make with the greatest deliberation.

༤ᏙᏙ༢

PAY ANY PRICE,
BEAR ANY BURDEN

"LINDSEY PREDICTED Iraq War Would Cost $100 to $200 Billion." It is a line that I refuse to put on my tombstone, but there is little doubt that it will be the lead in some of my obituaries. As things turned out, the estimate was far too low. But it was far higher than other estimates that were circulating around Washington at the time. For the last five years, whenever a reporter was around, despite my best efforts, the subject always came up. Washington teaches many ways to avoid answering a question you don't want to answer, and I've probably used them all to avoid publicly commenting on the issue. Until now. Here is the true story behind my estimate of the cost of the Iraq War.

On September 16, 2002, Bob Davis, a reporter for the *Wall Street Journal*, interviewed me in my West Wing office about what we had learned about the economic effects of the War on Terror in the year after 9/11. He then turned to the question of how one should assess the economics of eliminating potential terrorist threats, particularly Iraq. At the time, the administration was still pursuing the diplomatic route through the United Nations, and no decision had been made by the president to go to war.

There were two key economic points made in the article. The first was macroeconomic—the impact of a hypothetical war in Iraq on the deficit and interest rates. Many at the time were arguing that war costs would so balloon the deficit that it would drive up interest rates. They were arguing that taxes should be increased, a view that Davis privately shared. Davis sums up my comments as "Mr. Lindsey dismissed the economic consequences of such spending, saying it wouldn't have an appreciable effect on interest rates or add much to the federal debt, which is already about $3.6 trillion."[1] For the record, interest rates have remained low, and the federal deficit as a share of gross domestic product (GDP) is now smaller than it was then.

The second concern was microeconomic. Did a war in Iraq make sense from a cost–benefit point of view? The year after 9/11 proved the extent to which terrorism was a drag on the economy. We had already had to act to bail out the airline industry, propose reinsurance for downtown office structures, and begin spending tens of billions of dollars on increased homeland security. Markets were declining on fears of anthrax attacks and "dirty bombs" going off. Davis sums up my comment as "It's hard for me to see how we have sustained economic growth in a world where terrorists with weapons of mass destruction are running around. If you weigh the cost of the war against the removal of a huge drag on global economic growth for a foreseeable time in the future, there's no comparison."[2]

My point was clear. Even if a war in Iraq cost 1–2 percent of GDP ($100 billion to $200 billion at the time), a point he acknowledges in the article was a hypothetical "upper bound," it would still be worth it from an economic point of view. This is difficult for an economist who deals with figures all the time to admit, but when it comes to war, the dollar cost is hardly a major concern. Suppose Franklin Roosevelt's economic adviser had told him on December 8, 1941, that World War II was going to cost America 150 percent of its GDP, which it actually did. Would FDR have thought, "Well, the war is worth it at 130 percent of GDP but not at 170 percent"? Or suppose there had been a massive cost overrun and in the spring of 1945 Treasury Secretary Henry Morgenthau had told FDR that the war had already cost 300 percent of GDP. Would FDR have said, "In that case, let's call the whole thing off"? It is, of course, absurd to think that the rationale for preserving the United States would come down to such "pennywise, pound-foolish" calculations.

Economically, what matters in a war is whether you win or lose. It is as simple as that. If a country loses a war, the suffering of its people is virtually immeasurable. That is true even when you lose to a comparatively benign country like America. True, we did help rebuild Japan and Germany after World War II, but life in both of those countries in the late 1940s was hardly pleasant. Should, God forbid, America lose the war to Islamic fascism or some totalitarian power or even if one of our enemies should be able to destroy one of our cities with a weapon of mass destruction, no one would be talking about 1 percent, 2 percent, or even 50 percent of GDP.

This is not to say that an economic adviser shouldn't think about these things or that every effort shouldn't be made to estimate the cost of the war as accurately as possible. But the value of the analysis is indirect. If the job of an adviser is simply to answer the question "How fast will the economy grow next year?" he or she should simply write the number "3" on a piece of paper, leave it on his desk, and head to the golf course. On average, that is how fast the economy has been growing for decades and is a very defensible estimate of how fast it will grow in any given year in the future. Frankly, it also really doesn't matter much whether the economy grows 2.8 percent or 3.2 percent in any one year. No individual who was not glued to the statistics would even notice. The difference works out to an additional 40 cents of spending per person per day. Moreover, our statistical apparatus for even estimating the size of the economy has an error that large.

The two best questions that an economic policy adviser can think about are (1) is there anything on the horizon that *might* cause the economy to grow significantly slower than average? and (2) if there is such a threat on the horizon, is there something that can or should be done? Later in this book, we consider the bursting of the 1990s stock market bubble as a great example of such an event and that it took some long-term planning to mitigate the effects of the bubble's collapse. The response to the collapse of the bubble is an example of the kind of issue to which the answer to both of these questions is yes, making it the kind of issue that warranted attention.

Certainly in late 2002, it was worth considering the economic impact of a possible war in Iraq as one of those events that could conceivably derail the economy. By early November, the UN Security Council would vote 15 to 0 to tell Saddam Hussein that his continued noncompliance with UN legal resolutions would result in "serious consequences." That was diplomatic code for war. Saddam was showing no real signs of complying.

The economic recovery at the time was still fragile, so much so that I was actively agitating for an acceleration of the staggered tax cuts passed the previous year as a way of nurturing the economic recovery. So, a real shock to the economy from the war through high oil prices or diminished confidence would certainly be the kind of risk that could have meaningful economic consequences.

The economic effects of a possible war with Iraq therefore met the two criteria as something worthy of spending some time on. But implicit behind my comments to Davis, no matter how one calculated the purely *budgetary* cost of the war, it was hard to get a number that posed a significant threat to the recovery.

That was true using either historic comparisons or contemporary rules of thumb regarding force commitments. For example, the liberation of Kuwait in 1991 cost the equivalent of 1 percent of GDP at the time. The Iraq operation was likely to cost more but seemingly less than twice as much. The Vietnam War cost between

1.5 and 2 percent of GDP per year during the eight years of major American commitment. At its peak, we had over 500,000 members of our armed forces in Vietnam. We were going to have less than one-third as many in Iraq.

Alternatively, we were going to be putting between 7 and 10 percent of our total armed forces personnel in the country. With the war, our total defense budget would likely run between 4 and 5 percent of GDP, suggesting that merely by apportioning the share of our military expenditures to Iraq, we would be talking about a figure between one-third and one-half of 1 percent of GDP. This would understate the actual cost. Troops in a combat situation expend more resources than those not in combat. In addition, there would likely be a substantial amount of the logistical support and infrastructure rebuilding. So, based on these sorts of calculations, the most plausible number was that the cost of the war was going to be between 0.5 and 1 percent of GDP for each year that we were going to be involved in the conflict. A year near the high end of that range and one to two additional years of follow-up at the lower end produced a total cost of between 1 and 2 percent of GDP. As things turned out, Iraq itself is costing about seven-tenths of a percent of America's GDP per year, not terribly more than we spend on cosmetics and personal hygiene products like hair care each year, but the war has gone on longer than expected, so its cumulative cost is higher.

In addition, when one analyzes such costs, it is useful to compare them with an alternative. If those resources were suddenly not deployed in Iraq, it is not the case that they would be available to be spent on food, clothing, and education. Consider the phrase "phased redeployment," which is what Iraq war critics propose doing with the troops there now. The proposal is not to redeploy the troops from Iraq to America's farms to grow food or schools to become teachers. Rather, the proposal is to redeploy the troops to other overseas bases in places like Kuwait, Europe, and Asia, with some returning to bases in the United States. That means that the economic effect of the money involved was likely to be even smaller than the mere dollar amount suggested.

With this in mind, consider military expenditures from the big-picture economic perspective. The total cost of the American defense budget is less than 5 percent of GDP. That is well below the average defense burden in America for the past 100 years, especially when one takes into account that conscription artificially lowered the cost of defense in budgetary terms during much of this period. No matter how one looks at the purely budgetary facts of the Iraq War, it is hard to argue that it is terribly out of line with the American experience of the past hundred years. There are many aspects of the Iraq War worthy of a national debate. But for all the reasons mentioned here, the budget impact of the endeavor should be far down the list.

If war critics were therefore making too much about the dollar figure, the reaction within the White House was also well off the mark. The communications people were furious. The obvious criticism leveled at anyone who made news during that time was that it was "off message" or that "message discipline had been broken." Even in hindsight, I do not believe the message was inappropriate or even contrary to administration thinking. The interview stated that even if we had a war in Iraq, it would not put upward pressure on interest rates and would not derail the economy. That was true *even if* the war cost $100 billion to $200 billion. Moreover, whether the war cost $50 billion or $200 billion did not alter whether the war was "worth it" from a cost–benefit point of view.

Another criticism that was made of my comments internally was that the president had not decided to go to war and that therefore it was inappropriate to estimate the cost of such a decision. This really doesn't make a lot of sense to me. My son's fifth-grade class was discussing the possibility of going to war in Iraq. So, this wasn't the cost of some top-secret new weapons system or some secret mission that was being aired in the *Wall Street Journal*.

Candidly, the reason why the quote ended up making front-page news and not being buried on page 8 was that the entire country was talking about everything related to the Iraq War *except the White House.* If there was a break in message discipline, it was not that the actual words of the message were wrong; rather, it was that there was a message at all. At that time, message discipline on Iraq was the functional equivalent of radio silence.

Then there is the rather obvious good-government point about saying something about the cost of an idea the president may not follow through on. Should one wait until *after* the president has already decided to go to war before estimating the war's cost or economic impact? The idea is preposterous.

The real problem with the interview for my colleagues in the White House was not what was actually said but that it mentioned a hypothetical cost of the war that might be sufficiently high to raise budgetary objections in Congress. This thinking implied that it is better to give a lower-bound cost estimate because it is likely to raise fewer objections. This strategy is always wrong on two very important counts.

First, the White House strategy implicitly concedes the point that budgetary cost is a legitimate criterion for objecting to fighting the War on Terror in Iraq. We had just suffered $80 billion in damage and lost 3,000 lives from some terrorists flying planes into the World Trade Center and Pentagon. Money of this order of magnitude should not have been an issue even if one was purely a green-eye-shaded accountant.

More to the point, going to war is never an accounting issue. Forty years earlier, President John F. Kennedy had rallied the country saying that "we would pay any price, bear any burden, to assure the success and survival of liberty." It is not too much of a leap in logic that we would pay at least that much to also assure that the American people could go to work on beautiful September mornings without having to make the choice between being burned alive or jumping to their deaths from eightieth-story offices.

There were many important questions to debate about Iraq. Was this the right strategic move in our war on terror? Were the tactics we were going to employ ones that would lead to victory? But if it all came down to a public debate and the critics' best argument against the war is that it would cost $150 billion and not $50 billion, the president would have already won the debate.

The second reason the White House strategy was flawed was that simply providing a "best-case" cost estimate is neither good government nor good politics. The great strength of a democracy is its ability to settle issues by putting all the facts on the table. As noted, the budgetary cost of the war is hardly the most salient fact to be talking about, but the right thing to do is to be as honest and open as one can be on all issues, subject to the legitimate concerns of national security.

This is not to say that the people who put together a lower budget estimate were being dishonest. They may have legitimately thought that *the most likely* cost of the war was well under $100 billion. They should say so and say it that way. It is also true that no one could really know in advance what such a war would cost. That should be said explicitly as well. Real budgetary candor would involve giving a probability-weighted assessment of the costs that lay ahead and admitting that the range of likely outcomes was wide.

Faced with the uncertainty of war, good government involves making two points. The first is an assessment of a range of scenarios: best case, worst case, and most likely would be three good examples. The second is an argument that under almost any scenario that seems likely, the *war will be worth it, at least compared with the alternatives, if the war can be won.*

This approach is also good politics. Granted, "good politics" is in the eye of the beholder, but looking back on the whole incident, one would have to conclude that the path the administration took in commenting on the cost of the war did a disservice to the president. The fact that the actual cost of the war turned out to be even higher than 1 to 2 percent of GDP—because the war took a lot longer to fight than anyone expected—has led to a variety of criticisms of the president. Some say he lied. Some say he was incompetent. One hears these criticisms ad nauseam.

So, simply from the perspective of good *politics*, would it have cost the president more politically to have said that the war *might* cost $200 billion or to have the constant refrain about lies and incompetence? For the record, the president did not lie, nor was he incompetent. The president doubtless believed, based on the facts that were available to him at the time, that he was making the right decision with regard to toppling Saddam. It was also quite reasonable for him to conclude that the alternative strategies, most of which involved either leaving a substantial body of American forces near Iraq ready to invade if the facts warranted or living with a high degree of risk and uncertainty in a post-9/11 world, were not attractive.

But putting out only a best-case scenario without preparing the public for some worse eventuality was the wrong strategy to follow. It may have helped at the margin in the very short run by making the war sound more attractive. But this came at the expense of undermining the president's political capital in the long run. And the long run is when the president would need political capital the most. If things turn out better than expected, the president will be enormously popular, and the higher cost estimates will be irrelevant. No one ever complained if a government program came in under budget. But if things did happen to turn out worse than expected, the public would have to believe that this was due to unforeseen events and not that the president had somehow misled them.

The president needed his credibility to keep the American people focused on the long struggle we face against people who are out to kill us and destroy our way of life. How sad for the country and for the cause of freedom that this credibility was eroded by sticking to a budgetary cost estimate that turned out to be wrong.

So now you know the story behind my likely obituary. You also know why I feel so passionately about the next memo I left on the president's desk.

MEMORANDUM FOR THE PRESIDENT

FROM: LAWRENCE B. LINDSEY
SUBJECT: WAR IS HELL, FOR YOU
January 20, 2009

When it came to the issue of who was in charge of national policy in time of war, the Founding Fathers knew firsthand of what they wrote. The Continental Congress had tried to micromanage the conduct of the Revolutionary War, much to General Washington's frustration. At Valley Forge, on the verge of his crossing of the Delaware River to rout the British, Washington did the constitutionally unthinkable. He ignored the principle of the "power of the purse" and promised the men whose commissions were expiring a bonus for reenlisting even though he did not have Congress's authorization to do so, not to mention an appropriation to make good on the promise.

The Constitutional Convention ultimately made the president the commander in chief. Congress was given the power to declare war and the power to appropriate funds for defense but the latter with the condition that the appropriation not last for more than two years. This is hardly a mandate for micromanagement. Moreover, a declaration of war requires only a majority vote in both chambers, not a very high hurdle during a time of saber rattling. This meant that should the commander in chief seek to go to war, there would not be a lot of legislative logrolling or deal making needed to get such authorization.

Nonetheless, today an action by you like Washington's would be grounds for impeachment, and it certainly was grounds for Congress to remove Washington from his role as commander. But, Washington stayed on, and you would too, provided that the constitutionally elastic action you pulled off worked. This is not a recommendation for you to run roughshod over the Constitution, though as we shall see, many of your predecessors did. In war, even liberals like Lincoln, Wilson, and FDR trampled not just on marginal liberties but on some that anyone today would consider among our most essential. It is an observation that in your role as commander in chief nothing succeeds like success.

The main reason the Constitution functions in this practical and very elastic manner rather than in a legalistic one is that going to war is an act like no other. It places everything at risk. Lose a war, and our lives are changed forever, and our Constitution itself could disappear. Succeed, and the cause of liberty is advanced, and the truths on which our country was based become more universally applied around the world.

The second, largely operational reason for this conflict between liberty and the necessities of war is that America is among the most war-averse world powers in history. In part this is geographical; being surrounded by two oceans helps breed a false sense of security and a willingness to be detached from the world. In part this is demographic. A nation comprised of people from all over the world finds it nearly impossible to rally the nation around the principles of kith and kin or tribe or even culture that unify most nations. Making your enemy the "other," a nonhuman beast who deserves to be killed, is often thought of as essential to overcome qualms about killing him. We are a nation of "others." Finally, we are a culture of individualism, and war is the ultimate action of collectivism. For different reasons, both the broad-based American middle class and the academic and cultural elites tend to resist going to war.

This is all a good thing. It makes us the safest superpower in the history of the world. That may not be the fashionable opinion in the salons of Paris, London, or even the Upper West Side, but it is certainly true. For example, the president of France may deploy the French Foreign Legion wherever he chooses outside of France without any consultation with the French National Assembly. France regularly deploys its armed forces in its former African colonies without so much as a by-you-leave nod to the UN Security Council. The British Cabinet is presumed to have the authorization to act by Parliament, and Britain possesses an Official Secrets Act that permanently prohibits discussion of the documents relevant to war preparation in the media. And these are other democracies, not Russia, China, or Iran.

So, although you are the most powerful commander in chief on the planet, you are also the most constrained. This memorandum alerts you to those constraints and suggests how you might cope with them. **But before delving into the details, here's one word of purely personal advice about going to war: DON'T. It is bound to kill you, either physically or politically**. Lincoln, Wilson, FDR, and Lyndon Johnson either died in office or shortly thereafter or aged in office as a direct consequence of the wars they fought. Nixon and your immediate predecessor were politically ruined by war, and, in the case of Bush, aged enormously as a consequence of his decision.

But you didn't become president in order to live a long life. You did so to make a difference. Here is a list of the constraints you will be under should fate require you to take this nation to war:

THE CONSTRAINT OF YOUR TIME AND ATTENTION

This is the most subtly pernicious of the constraints because you invariably will not see it coming. It is also the most deadly, both physically and politically. Going to war requires you, as commander in chief, to make and supervise a whole range of decisions that simply cannot be delegated successfully. It also requires a host of ceremonial functions that will also drain your time. These range from far more diplomatic meetings with allies and potential allies to the need to review troops and visit those who have suffered grievous injuries in the hospital. The latter are physically and emotionally draining.

You, with the active involvement of your chief of staff, will be engaging in time triage: things you can't delegate and things you can easily delegate will become automatic, leaving the tough calls in the middle. One item that can't be delegated but may fall through the cracks is your physical and mental health. Lincoln likely chose to go to Ford's Theater because he felt he needed a night out. April 1865 had been tough on him, filled with decisions about how to bring about the end of the Confederacy without provoking the defeated army into going to the mountains to conduct a protracted guerilla war. Today, with both war and history moving at an even faster pace, every month will be like that. And while modern versions of John Wilkes Booth will be kept away from your precious moments off, the press will not, providing pictures of you on the golf course or the beach while soldiers are dying.

RECOMMENDATION: If you go to war, take breaks anyway. You are a workaholic by nature, so your instincts about needing a vacation are invariably right, not frivolous. Fewer soldiers will die if you are making good decisions and the country needs you to be mentally healthy and alert.

The other part of your job that time triage will place at risk is your non-war related decision making. Standard operating procedure within the West Wing will be, "We are at war, don't bother the president with that." It is a sound notion and well intentioned. But as the war drags on, it is a recipe for isolation and becoming out of touch with the country's mood. This will hurt your standing politically and therefore may ultimately limit your flexibility as commander in chief.

One historical example of this was the congressional midterm elections of 1942. Memories of Pearl Harbor were still quite real, and millions of American troops were already deployed overseas. If ever there were to be a "rally round the flag" election, this would be it. But the opposition Republicans gained forty-seven seats in the House and nine in the Senate. They actually outpolled the Democrats in House races by five percentage points and failed to gain outright control of the House only because of the "solid South." The Roosevelt administration had lost touch with the national mood, gambling that patriotism would trump all other issues. A prime example of this was the announcement before Election Day that coffee rationing would begin. One can only suspect, given how savvy a politician FDR was, that the coffee decision never even crossed his desk.

But the pitfalls of isolation are more than just political. There are a variety of trade-offs that only the president can make. For example, to what extent should domestic air travel be curtailed in order to facilitate the movement of manpower and material overseas? During the

Cold War, one of the reasons for developing the nation's civil aviation system was to provide a backup airlift capability for the resupply and reinforcement of our forces in Europe. Nearly all the pilots were ex-military. Foreign ownership of American airlines was prohibited. It was assumed that the entire civilian air fleet could be commandeered in a war. But not only today but even as early as the 1970s, such a commandeering would have had an almost crippling effect on the domestic economy. It would not take long for that to spill over into the war effort. Unless the president is receiving regular input from his domestic and economic advisers as well as his foreign policy brain trust, his ability to make trade-offs like this will be impaired.

RECOMMENDATIONS: First, you will need to delegate as many economic and domestic policy judgments as possible to an adviser or small group of advisers who you completely trust and who share your sense of priorities. Ideally, they should be people who can internalize your worldview and simply overlay their technical expertise on top. Second, you will need to allocate some time each week to meet with these people alone to hear about and respond to the judgments they have made. In addition, you should set time aside at least monthly to meet with people they recommend from across the country. The purpose of these meetings primarily will be for you to listen and not to be a persuader.

THE CONSTRAINT OF THE
GOVERNMENT BUREAUCRACY

When you pay your first visit to the Eisenhower Executive Office Building next door, take a look at the doorknobs. There will be three types: one with an anchor, one with an eagle with outstretched wings, and one with a shield with crossed swords and arrows. Prior to World War II, this Victorian-era wedding cake of a building, then simply called the Executive Office Building, housed the Navy Department, State Department, and War Department. The doorknobs indicate which department held which office.

Now of course, the War Department and Navy Department have expanded to fill the Pentagon, which remains the largest single office building in the world. The State Department occupies an eight-story structure that occupies an entire city block. To this, a third bureaucracy has been added, the Central Intelligence Agency (CIA), which was created after World War II and has its own sprawling complex across the river in Virginia at Langley. To attempt to get a handle on all this, another, much smaller bureaucracy was added: the National Security Council, headed by an assistant to the president, your national security adviser. This much smaller group now occupies part of the West Wing and about one-quarter of the Executive Office Building that used to house all of War, State, and Navy.

On an organization chart, all these people work for you. To be generous, this actually occurs only with significant effort on your part. In 1963, Jerry Pournelle coined the phrase "Iron Law of Bureaucracy," which states that in any organization there are two types of people—those devoted to the mission of the organization and those devoted to the organization itself—and that the latter gradually gains power over the former.[3] But similar sentiments were expressed early on by Balzac in the early nineteenth century and by Marx later in that century. Suffice it to say that political theory across the spectrum says that the deck is stacked against you when it comes to controlling the bureaucracy.

There are two separate challenges involved. First, the bureaucratic self-interest of each organization is to preserve the status quo, that is, avoid going to war. That is actually probably the right call most of the time, but if you decide the opposite, you should not expect these organizations to fall in line. The rationale of the State Department may be the most obvious. By definition, the State Department prefers diplomacy. While its mission is to represent American interests abroad, cynics often note that its real function is to represent foreign interests to America. Even to the extent that these cynics are right, that is not entirely a bad thing, as the State Department provides a useful sounding board for the likely international response to any decision you make.

As a bureaucracy though, State has another reason to oppose going to war. War strips away all the illusions and ambiguous assumptions about one's diplomatic counterparts that actually allows a well-balanced individual to function as a diplomat. Secretary Colin Powell certainly discovered that about French Foreign Minister Dominique de Villepin just before the start of the Iraq War. No individual or organization likes to have its worldview, even one it knows intellectually to be somewhat artificial, simply swept away.

The CIA has a similar antiwar bias and for similar reasons. The CIA traffics in knowing something that others cannot know because of the opaqueness of other, potentially hostile societies. In a war, particularly after a victory, the former society becomes transparent, and so the quality of the CIA's product becomes open for all to evaluate. For example, after the successful invasion of Iraq, it was obvious that CIA Director George Tenet's assertion that Saddam Hussein possessed weapons of mass destruction was something less than a "slam dunk."

After the fall of the Berlin Wall, we learned that decades of CIA assertions about the growth rate of the Soviet economy were mathematically implausible. The CIA once erroneously reported that per capita income in East Germany was higher than in West Germany. The problem was the use of different exchange rate conversions for the two countries. But anyone who had ever compared a Trabant with a Mercedes would have caught the mistake right away.

These were embarrassing gaffes. Both Iraq and the end of the Cold War led to reorganizations of the intelligence structure and in the latter case to a deemphasis of intelligence. The Iraq situation led to retaliation by CIA personnel. A senior career official at the CIA purportedly leaked information to the *Washington Post* about secret prisons. There were also leaks made about selected portions of intelligence reports that led to stories critical of the Bush administration. This is a normal part of bureaucratic covering of exposed rear ends. Whatever the merits of the particulars, this is not a behavior that you would want to have happen during your administration.

The antiwar bias of the Pentagon is by far the least intuitive. The standard view in the intellectual salons and higher echelons of the media is that the place is packed with testosterone-driven warmongers. In fact, many of the senior decision makers in the military did engage in truly heroic feats of bravery during their careers. But today, those decision makers are in their late forties and fifties. These are people with families, mortgages, and pensions on their mind, people who proved their courage in battle decades earlier.

War costs the lives of the men and women that these decision makers have worked with and know personally. That is far more the case at the Pentagon than at any other institution in Washington. And while the military ethic acknowledges these deaths as part of the cost of preserving liberty, that doesn't make advocating the deaths of friends a preferred alternative.

There are also more cynical theories floating around for the military aversion to war. Careers get ruined by mistakes. Procurement programs that military leaders have advocated actually get tested and are often proved to be failures, creating a careerist problem like the ones at State and the CIA. But the fact remains that when it comes to describing the attitude at the Pentagon, "Peace through Strength" is an infinitely more accurate moniker than "Warmonger."

There is a final point to make about these bureaucracies. Not only do they have their own interests, but they are not shy about fighting each other to place blame when the going gets rough. A recent example of this occurred in your predecessor's administration and helped to cripple its effectiveness. During the debate over Iraq policy, the deputy secretary of state, Richard Armitage, made a mistake that resulted in a newspaper column that proved embarrassing to the administration. The president publicly asked for the identity of the perpetrator, and ultimately a special prosecutor was named. Neither the actual source of the column nor his boss, the secretary of state, told the president, their boss, what had happened. Instead, the actual perpetrator cooperated with the prosecutor, with the public blame ultimately falling on his bureaucratic enemies within the administration.

Whatever your view of the issues or the individuals involved, you certainly would not want this to happen in your administration. Nor should you. No manager in any institution would or should tolerate behavior that is both insubordinate and so detrimental to others in the institution. But you are not any manager, and the bureaucracies you oversee are not any bureaucracies. Hence some special recommendations for your special circumstances:

RECOMMENDATIONS: First, take entrenched bureaucratic opposition to your plans as a signal that you are not going to succeed. There is of course the obvious possibility that the bureaucracy may be right. But even if they are not right on the merits, this kind of opposition greatly increases the chance that you will not succeed. You will be spending too much of your time, energy, and political capital on the battles within your own administration and not enough on winning the war.

Second, there is probably an exception to this general rule we could call the Valley Forge exception. Like General Washington, you can roll the opposition simply by acting decisively and winning quickly. This rules out most protracted campaigns, but if you can achieve your objectives within, say, ninety days, the internal bureaucratic opposition will not have time to take effective countermeasures.

Third, you should seek individuals with strong managerial talents for the tops of these organizations. This means, at a minimum, having either the secretary or the deputy secretary spend the bulk of his or her days managing and attempting to control the bureaucracy. In Washington this is called "adult supervision." The bureaucracy will try and co-opt the "short timer" overseeing it the same way a group of siblings try to run over a babysitter. The supervision you hire must be top quality.

Once you've got your own administration lined up to support you, the hard part begins.

THE CONSTRAINT OF PUBLIC SUPPORT

As noted earlier, America is the safest superpower in the history of the world precisely because Americans are not easily persuaded to go to war. Many of the institutional constraints discussed above are man-ifestations of that. Getting and keeping public support for your war effort is one of the aspects of your job as commander in chief that you cannot delegate to others. It will be the biggest drain on your time and energies.

RECOMMENDATION: From the beginning, don't lowball the amount of sacrifice that will be needed.

Putting in too low a cost estimate for the Iraq War was one of the tactical blunders of the Bush administration. By and large, with respect to the general war against Islamic terrorism, the president and the administration stressed the long-term nature of the struggle. So the Iraq cost estimate is a bit of an outlier, yet that one point is used over and over again as evidence of the administration's effort to build support for the war by understating its cost, thus undermining its credibility.

But even giving them the benefit of the doubt, the administration certainly has not risen to Churchillian levels in talking about the sac-rifices needed. When he became prime minister, Winston Churchill promised about what lies ahead: "I have nothing to offer but blood, toil, tears, and sweat." And when the tide had clearly turned, he was not given to euphoria. "It is not the beginning of the end, but it is, per-haps, the end of the beginning." And history certainly shows that Churchill knew how to lead a free people in war.

No one will ever blame you if the war is easier to win than you thought it would be or if it comes in under budget. This leads auto-matically to the next recommendation:

RECOMMENDATION: Do what it takes to get it over with as quickly as possible.

From a military perspective, this comes down to the Powell Doc-trine, named after former Secretary of State and Chairman of the Joint Chiefs of Staff Colin Powell. It is also sometimes called the Doctrine of Overwhelming Force. At its root, it comes down to a single funda-mental principle of decision theory that anyone can grasp: why take a chance when you don't have to?

The one clear advantage that America has against most of its foes is our potential to both outman them and outspend them. By some modes of analysis, America spends more on defense than all the other countries in the world combined. (Note that this is not the same as saying that we have a stronger military than all the other countries in the world combined or could win a war against them. Military power is a much more complicated metric than that.) But against any single foe, we possess overwhelming superiority.

The Powell Doctrine will help in two ways. First, it is the most certain way of getting the support of the bureaucracy, particularly the Pentagon. As noted, this is one of the key bureaucracies in Washington that you need, and this is one of their articles of faith. It also helps indirectly in getting the support of the two other key bureaucracies by appealing to their core sets of values. The intelligence community is fundamentally an evaluator of risk, with an appropriate preference for less risky endeavors. When the country is about to make a commitment of massive force, the risks go down. This does not eliminate their other reasons for caution, but it does reduce them. The same is true of the Foreign Service. It still may have a strong preference for doing things diplomatically, but if the country is going to war anyway, it clearly would rather the country win. It is far better being the diplomatic representative of a winning superpower than one that is bogged down somewhere in a country one-tenth its size.

The second benefit of the Powell Doctrine is that it reduces the amount of time the war is likely to take and therefore the amount of time that you, as commander in chief, will have to maintain public support. Typically, American support for war is intense at the beginning, driven by outrage at the causus belli that mobilizes the country to go to war. It diminishes as the sacrifices accumulate in terms of body bags or lower levels of the comforts of home.

Moreover, as time drags on, mistakes are more likely to be made, and those mistakes that are made are increasingly likely to be aired in public. Our soldiers are well trained and disciplined, but discipline does snap under pressure, and judgment calls about battlefield risks create incidents that critics can characterize as "massacres." Worse, commanders do make mistakes, and our enemies are not without talent. Battlefield defeats will occur, and this saps public support.

As General Washington discovered after Valley Forge, nothing succeeds like success. As time passes, patience wanes, and the perception of success is harder to maintain. But, once again, when it comes to maintaining public support for a war, Churchill said it best: "It is no use saying 'We are doing our best.' You have got to succeed in doing what is necessary."

Still, even doing it as quickly as possible will probably not be enough.

RECOMMENDATION: Call it propaganda if you like but realize at the beginning that you are going to need a sustained and intense communications effort that defines for America why we are doing what we are doing. Moreover, your effort had better be quite close to the truth.

Sometimes you will just get lucky but don't count on it. The best example of luck happened in October 1983. President Ronald Reagan had decided to invade the small Caribbean island of Grenada, which had just had a coup led by a pro-Soviet and pro-Cuban faction that led to the execution of Prime Minister Maurice Bishop. Reagan's efforts to fight the Cold War in the Western Hemisphere were decidedly unpopular among many American elites who were sympathetic to the left in Latin America. Media coverage was decidedly skeptical.

Then a planeload of American students who were attending St. George's University in Grenada were airlifted off the island by the military and landed at a base in the United States. The media were covering the event live, seeking to interview the students with the expectation that the promises by the pro-Soviet Grenadian government that they were never in any danger were accurate. One of the first students off the plane got down on his knees and kissed the tarmac. Opposition to the invasion simply vanished. No one could compete with the image of an American kissing American soil in thanks for his rescue. *Symbolism matters.*

It is useful to consider just how lucky the Reagan administration was with this image. *Even if* the sentiments of the student were an accurate reflection of the situation, the odds that an American would spontaneously create such a vivid image were small. Moreover, the administration got lucky that the press was there to cover the event live. The picture itself could easily have ended up on the cutting-room floor if some hostile editor had control of the process. But millions of Americans were watching live and were curious. You should not count on such luck.

The best aspect of this event from the administration's point of view was that the coverage of the event was entirely in the hands of the media, and therefore its genuineness could not be questioned. In World War I and World War II, the administrations went out of their way to force-feed the public propaganda that supported the cause, and it is useful to review the extent of those efforts. But the modern media (and probably even the media back then) do not like to be controlled. It is always best, if possible, to simply present the facts and let them take it from there.

An outstanding example of this process occurred during the early stages of the Iraq War. The media were skeptical, if not hostile. The military, breaking with tradition, decided to embed reporters in the actual units doing the fighting. Moreover, those reporters were uplinking their coverage directly to satellites and thereby giving live coverage of the fighting. Some thought the military was taking a big risk. If one of those units committed what might look like a massacre or atrocity or was on the receiving end of some horrific attack with poison gas (which many were expecting), there would be exactly the wrong image being conveyed.

The only restriction on the reporters' live coverage was that they not take a camera shot that would convey the actual position of the unit. After all, a live camera shot was being broadcast all around the world, including to the enemy. It should be noted that this also coincided with the reporters' own self-interest in that if mortar fire were called down on the unit, they would be in as much danger as anyone else.

But this self-interest on the part of reporters was actually the basis of the brilliance of the whole communications effort. There is nothing like having people shooting at you to convey who the good guys are and who the bad guys are. The message was not entirely positive, nor could any live and uncensored reporting possibly have been in any war. Some of the units ran short of rations. Some needed better body armor or more ammunition. This built the case that the administration was not doing enough to support the troops. On the other hand, it is certainly not a public relations defeat when you clearly identify who the good guys are and that the good guys need even more support from back home. Another drawback occurred when some of the units ran short of gasoline and had to stop; the case was made in the anchor rooms that "the war was bogging down." The latter point disappeared when Baghdad was taken in a far quicker amount of time than even the optimistic estimates.

The more difficult lesson came later when we discovered that our enemies can play the same game. Gunfights were set up with cameras pre-positioned to make it look like American forces were shooting at ambulances, for example. Moreover, when our troops do make mistakes, which they inevitably will, places like Abu Ghraib will be festooned all over the world's media for months. That is all the more reason why you will need to set up an intense and creative communications operation on a full-time basis. Our enemies certainly will.

RECOMMENDATION: Clearly define the enemy. But remember that in so doing, you too will be defined.

Sociologists note that defining your enemy as being "different" or somehow subhuman is an integral part of developing acceptance of the killing of them. The phrase is making them the "other." This is something that runs counter to our values and the universal truths on which our nation was founded, such as "all men are created equal, that they are endowed by their creator . . ." That means our enemies too. It is even harder given that we are a nation of immigrants, some of whom may be the brothers, sisters, and cousins of "others."

But when the chips were down, this didn't stop your predecessors, all of whom appreciated the value of propaganda. Lincoln may have been the most conflicted since the "other" was fellow Americans. When he met Harriet Beecher Stowe, author of *Uncle Tom's Cabin*, he reportedly said, "so this is the little lady who made this big war," acknowledging her role in defining the enemy.

President Woodrow Wilson was far clearer about the Germans. He created a Committee on Public Information, the main arm of which was a group known as Four Minute Men, who gave more than 750,000 speeches that defined the enemy around the country. Public speaking by this sort of "team" was the only form of mass communication available in an age before either radio or television. They worked with the American Protective League, a 250,000-strong organization that tapped telephones and opened mail. (So much for the Constitution.) But it is in the use of Hollywood that the creation of the "other" is clearest. Some of the titles of the day were *The Claws of the Hun*, *The Prussian Cur*, and *The Kaiser: The Beast of Berlin*. No subtlety here.

Wilson's situation was delicate. Germany was then (and still is) the largest single ancestral homeland to Americans. They are a key voting bloc in the Midwest, the swing region that helps decide most American elections, and a region geographically inclined to be isolationist. After a particularly nasty battle in 1916, the leading newspaper of the region, the *Chicago Tribune*, ran the isolationist headline "Thank God for Columbus!" Moreover, Wilson confronted another large ethnic group, the Irish, whose ancestral homeland was in rebellion against one of our would-be allies, Great Britain. Cognizant of that, Wilson ran for reelection on the theme that "he kept us out of the war." Wilson's instincts on this were correct. After the war, the nation turned against his party, particularly in the Midwest, turning instead to a neoisolationist "Return to Normalcy."

But during the actual American involvement, political realities did not stop Wilson from a major propaganda effort. Indeed, it may have been these political facts of life that made an overwhelming propaganda effort necessary. Those same realities may have driven him to a major crackdown on domestic dissent, the details of which are described shortly.

President Franklin Roosevelt had the benefit of Wilson's experience. Although decidedly pro-British, he knew he could not easily rally an isolationist country to war, deciding instead to co-opt potential opponents and keeping the political debate focused on his strong suit: economic revival. He appointed a leading Irish American, Joseph Kennedy, to be ambassador to Britain, limiting political exposure on that front. Moreover, Kennedy was decidedly pro-German and anti-Semitic and feared that Churchill was leading Roosevelt into the war. He finally had to resign in November 1940 after Roosevelt's reelection. But even after Pearl Harbor, Roosevelt did not ask for a declaration of war against Germany—Germany obliged with a declaration of war against America—and the war's propaganda effort was turned toward a more easily definable and less politically risky "other," namely, the Japanese.

Japan had been a nominal ally during World War I and was developing in a modestly democratic direction until the Depression. That did not stop the academy from turning out books at the start of the war that defined Japanese people and culture as inherently warlike based on the samurai ethic known as Bushido. A look back at the mass culture of the period shows a real effort to concoct the "other" as bloodthirsty and subhuman. One famous poster shows a grotesque and satanic-looking Japanese soldier walking away with a woman—who just happened to be white—slung over his shoulder. The more typical image of Japanese in the art of the time was as monkeys. One poster showed an ape labeled "Japan" with a gun labeled "civilization" pointed at his head.

Hollywood fully cooperated in the effort. The 1943 Academy Award for Best Documentary went to Frank Capra's *Prelude to War*, the first feature in the Why We Fight series. It showed a Japanese army marching down Pennsylvania Avenue as the voice-over says, "You will see what they did to the men and women of Nanking, Hong

Kong, and Manila. Imagine the field day they'd enjoy if they marched through the streets of Washington." Capra juxtaposed old samurai movies with actual war documentary footage to enhance the sense of realism. The film was acclaimed for its objectivity and was given its Oscar as a documentary.

Certainly, Japanese behavior in China and later in the Philippines did nothing to dispel the notion of Japanese savagery. But it is hard to argue that the Japanese were particularly more savage than their German allies. After all, a nation that develops a systematic high-tech extermination program for millions of people definitely sets a low bar in this regard. But anti-German propaganda during the war never reached the intensity or the racial characterization of the anti-Japanese propaganda.

December 7, 1941, certainly deserves to live as a Day of Infamy, but so do November 9, 1938, known as Kristallnacht, and August 23, 1939, the day the Russians and Germans partitioned Poland under the Molotov–von Ribbentrop Pact. They were not so labeled and didn't even result in a break in diplomatic relations. For propaganda to work, it must convey the "other" as doing something totally unthinkable. German actions simply did not outrage Americans sufficiently. In fact, just four months before Kristallnacht, Ambassador Kennedy met with the German ambassador to London, Herbert Von Dirksen. Von Dirksen reported to Berlin that Kennedy had told him that "it was not so much the fact that we want to get rid of the Jews that was so harmful to us, but rather the loud clamor with which we accompanied this purpose. [Kennedy] himself understood our Jewish policy completely."[4]

The Japanese were particularly stigmatized because, at the time, race politics made it easier, and it was considered a necessary part of the war effort. Our purpose here is not to pass judgment on these actions but to illustrate that in war you too may likely be forced to make similar judgments. The judgments you make, like these of Wilson and Roosevelt, will doubtless look even worse when viewed through the lens of history. Your predecessors made these calls not because they particularly wanted to but because they felt they had to. In war, ugly things tend to happen.

This is what presidents in wartime do in extremis. Even men who are enlightened for their times—and both Wilson and Roosevelt fit that description—make decisions that do not look so attractive from a historical perspective. **At a minimum, the need to create the "other" necessitates a double standard that historically will make you look like a hypocrite.** Bear in mind that some in the world equate American and British actions at Hiroshima and Dresden as comparable to the horrors perpetrated by the Germans and Japanese. Most reasonable men and women would not. But if you do not have the stomach to take the chance of going where these men ultimately went, you would be well advised not to march down the road to war in the first place.

And it is not just the commander in chief who let pragmatism trump conscience. As we shall see, some of the most renowned advocates of liberty and liberalism did so as well.

THE CONSTRAINT OF THE CONSTITUTION

If defining the enemy abroad, you may also find that you have defined part of your own country as a potential fifth column. We are an open country with immigrants from nearly every country on the planet and numerous visitors from them as well. That fact may be a particular challenge in any possible war that you may fight because one of our most likely enemies is Islamic fascism. Today, over 1 million Muslim adults live in America. Most are clearly not potential enemies or even sympathetic to Islamic fascism, and if they were, your ability to conduct a war would be severely hampered. But that also does not change the fact that some of these people (and some of any ethnic group derived from immigrants of a potential enemy) may pose a security risk. Your predecessors faced similar risks, and their behavior is unlikely to be the kind that you would want to emulate.

RECOMMENDATION: Enforce the laws vigorously against individuals but resist the temptation to abrogate our essential constitutional rights on a collective basis.

The classic case of collective abrogation of our constitutional rights came during World War II with the internment of American citizens of Japanese descent. On May 3, 1942, the general commanding the West Coast of the United States ordered that all persons of Japanese descent be evacuated to detention centers by May. In 1944, the Supreme Court decided, in *Korematsu v. United States*, that the law was constitutional by finding that a man who did not report, one Fred Korematsu, was lawfully convicted.

The case is interesting because no evidence was presented that Korematsu was a security risk, a fact acknowledged by the Court. His guilt under the law was simply determined by his ethnicity. It is also interesting that two of the court's more conservative jurists, Owen Roberts and Robert Jackson, dissented, while one of its most noted liberals, Hugo Black, wrote the majority opinion.

The opinion itself seems Orwellian from the perspective of six decades after the event. "We cannot reject as unfounded the judgment of the military authorities and of Congress that there were disloyal members of that population, whose number and strength could not be precisely and quickly ascertained." It then goes on, "Exclusion of those of Japanese origin was deemed necessary because of the presence of an unascertained number of disloyal members of the group, most of whom we have no doubt were loyal to this country. It was because we could not reject the finding of the military authorities that it was impossible to bring about an immediate segregation of the disloyal from the loyal that we sustained the validity of the curfew order as applying to the whole group."[5]

In other words, any individual is subject to detention, even though he is innocent, because he is a member of a group, most of whose members are also acknowledged to be innocent but some of whom may be guilty. Under this criterion any individual may be detained and subject to internal deportation at any time. But during World War II, it was not applied to German Americans or Italian Americans. It was a direct application of the concept of "other" in the conduct of the war to the domestic situation.

Today, the risks also run in reverse. By continuing to judge things on a racial basis, the courts have converted the notion that it was constitutionally permissible to detain an entire population based on ethnicity, to making it wrong if statistical analysis shows that you have stopped and questioned people of a given ethnicity proportionately more than the population at large. So today, even profiling people to determine who should be subject to a search before boarding an airplane is considered wrong. As a consequence, eighty-year-old grandmothers have their nail files confiscated, and no person is allowed to pack shampoo in their carry-on bags. History suggests that balance and reasonableness in either direction is not likely to be provided by the courts; the so-called living Constitution is so alive that it can metamorphose into totally unrecognizable shapes. It will be up to you to place a limit on the desire by those under you to make their lives easier by segmenting American citizens into groups of "others" for unconstitutional treatment.

RECOMMENDATION: You need not and should not go as far as your predecessors. But there is a trade-off for avoiding collective abrogation of constitutional rights as in World War II; it is a more vigorous monitoring of risks on an individual basis.

It is useful to consider just how far the nation has been prepared to abrogate individual constitutional rights like free speech in wartime. Our recent experience with wars in Vietnam and the Persian Gulf involved virtually no suppression of individual rights in contrast with the past. Peace marches and criticism of the government continued unhindered during these conflicts. In the past, presidents have confused genuine threats to the nation and political threats to their policies. Lincoln, for example, suspended the writ of habeas corpus and jailed critics of the war. But a more useful model of the risks to liberty is provided by President Woodrow Wilson.

Wilson provides the model of a supposedly liberal man completely abandoning some of the most fundamental of all liberties. At the start of World War I, he secured the passage of two of the more liberty-restricting acts of U.S. history. The Espionage Act and the Sedition Act made it illegal to oppose the draft or "willfully utter, print, write, or publish any disloyal, profane, scurrilous, or abusive language about the form of government of the United States, or the Constitution of the United States, or the military . . . or willfully utter, print, write, or publish any language intended to incite, provoke, or encourage resistance to the United States, or to promote the cause of its enemies." Violations were punishable by up to twenty years in jail, and the postmaster general was empowered to seize material in violation of the acts. (*New York Times* readers today would certainly be wondering what happened to their subscription under a similar law.) Presidential candidate Eugene Debs was imprisoned under the acts, along with more than 2,000 others. Debs had garnered 6 percent of the vote in his 1912 race against Wilson.

In Wilson's day, a request for a suspicious book was sufficient by itself to trigger an investigation. In fact, Attorney General Thomas Gregory demanded that the Librarian of Congress report the names of those who asked for specific titles.[6] Note that this is totally opposite from the standard law enforcement procedure of today in which a library card or record of movie rentals can be requested *after* an investigation has started for other reasons and only with the permission of a U.S. foreign intelligence surveillance court.

Nor was law enforcement done solely through standard channels in which the law enforcement agency was subject to oversight. Wilson did not feel that the limited resources of the federal government were sufficient to enforce these laws. The American Protective League, with the blessing of the Justice Department, recruited over 250,000 volunteers to help enforce the acts. Government posters urged people to report the man "who spreads pessimistic stories, divulges—or seeks—confidential military information, *cries for peace*, or belittles our efforts to win the war."[7]

Wilson had no qualms about this and certainly never admitted that there is a legitimate case for dissent. To the contrary, his view was that he had a moral obligation to crush dissent. In the run-up to war, Wilson said, "There are citizens of the United States, I blush to admit . . . who have poured the poison of disloyalty into the very arteries of our national life. . . . Such creatures of passion, disloyalty, and anarchy must be crushed out."[8]

It may be comforting to think that you would never become a Wilson or even a Roosevelt in the area of civil liberties during war. You may reason that the nation has changed. But as we saw in the previous chapter, there are those who work for you who, for the finest of motives, will feel differently. Technically, FDR did not order the imprisonment of the Japanese; a local military commander did. **But the most remarkable fact about a study of past presidents in wartime is how fast the values on which people make judgments change when the nation is endangered.**

Nor is it the case that the usually assumed constraints on these changes—the Constitution and the courts—will do their job. Rather, the most likely determiner of the extent to which civil liberties are abrogated will be you. History also suggests that your political persuasion is not likely to be a good predictor of your actual behavior. The trade-off will be personal: expediency for you and those who work for you versus liberty for others. Before you go to war, look in your heart to know what decision you will make. Then decide whether you will want your place in history to be determined by that decision. War will age you physically and hurt you politically, but if you are not careful, it will also kill any chances you have of going down in history as a president with a deep abiding faith in our civil liberties.

CHAPTER

FOUR

꧁

ENGAGING THE ENEMY

W AR IS A TEST of wills and resources between
countries. But it is also personal. In our own
lives, although we try not to dwell on the mat-
ter, we rarely forget who insulted us, who slighted us, or, who made
us lose face, especially if it happens in public. This is only human,
and we all understand this when it happens to us.

In something so important as war we expect our leaders to be
dispassionate and analytical. War is filled with more passion and
more moral outrage than the conflicts of our daily lives. After all,
if the result is a lot of dead bodies, there better be a good reason to
fight.

While some historians try to convey war merely as a fight
between countries or peoples or cultures, it is rarely convincing.
Roosevelt, Churchill, Hitler, and Stalin were inseparable from the
nations they led in World War II and even personally embodied
those nations in how other nations described them. The European
wars of the early nineteenth century are called the Napoleonic
Wars for a very good historic reason. It doubtless was always so in
history. Far more people have heard of Attila the Hun than can
identify the part of the world he came from, and certainly the Huns

would never have built an empire without him. The same was true of Alexander and Macedonia. Carthage may have been a great Mediterranean power in its day, but today few could place it on a map, yet most people have heard of Hannibal's famous crossing of the Alps.

This is because a nation needs a leader to take it into war. Lesser statesmen may go to war for light and trivial causes, even personal ones. A wise leader may try every way possible not to do so but may fail in the end. But even the wisest leader cannot separate himself or his feelings completely from the war effort of the nation he leads.

One presidential example of the human element at work in history is when John F. Kennedy met with Soviet leader Nikita Sergeyevich Khrushchev in 1961. At the time, Khrushchev thought Kennedy was weak and treated him badly. Kennedy later described the event in very personal terms: "Worst thing in my life. He savaged me. I think I know why he treated me like this. He thinks because of the Bay of Pigs . . . I have no guts." Kennedy went on to say, "We have to confront them. The only place we can do that is Vietnam."[1] It didn't take very long for a verbal confrontation between two men to lead to a consideration of conflict in a region far away. While this personal confrontation between Kennedy and Khrushchev was not the sole cause of the Vietnam War, it did help set the stage for war.

But the interaction was geopolitical as well as personal. Kennedy was right about the reason for Khrushchev's aggression. After their meeting that day in Vienna, the Soviet premier wondered to his assistants whether anyone who had abandoned his forces on the beaches of Cuba would have the stomach to launch a nuclear attack. He also allegedly asked the president of Westinghouse later at a meeting, "How can I deal with a man who is younger than my son?"[2]

Kennedy was also right to worry about his loss of face in public. After Vienna, Kennedy flew to London to consult with Prime Minister Harold Macmillan. In a note to Queen Elizabeth after the meeting, Macmillan wrote, "The President was completely overwhelmed by the ruthlessness and barbarity of the Russian chairman. It reminded me in a way of Lord Halifax or Neville Chamberlain trying to hold a conversation with Herr Hitler. . . . For the first time in his life Kennedy met a man who was impervious to his charm." Macmillan was even more direct in his diary, where he wrote, "I feel in my bones that President Kennedy is going to fail to produce any real leadership."[3] So even though Kennedy was taking the confrontation personally, he had solid geopolitical reasons for doing so.

Leaders naturally evaluate each other on a personal basis because it is the personality of the leader that will in large part determine the will of the country to fight. This is what Macmillan worried about since Kennedy was not only president of the United States but also leader of the free world. In the end, although the road to Vietnam had been laid, in Kennedy's mind it was the Cuban missile crisis that reestablished his bona fides as a leader. Khrushchev exploited his feelings about Kennedy's inadequacy by attempting to locate nuclear missiles in its newly established Cuban satellite, just ninety miles from American shores. This act clearly upset the security assumptions of the time since it opened the possibility of a surprise attack with insufficient warning for America to craft a coherent response. Kennedy knew he could not back down this time and instituted a blockade in the Atlantic, thereby threatening to go to war. This was just seventeen years after the end of World War II. The horrors of that war, coupled with regular and recurring aboveground nuclear tests, were fresh in the public's mind as they envisioned history's first confrontation between two superpowers armed with nuclear weapons. It is certainly sobering that the world was brought to the brink of nuclear war because of a meeting between two leaders that produced personal embarrassment for one of them.

I remember the period, having been about eight at the time. The local lumberyard had a display of prefabricated bomb shelters out front. While my parents were busy buying what they needed, I spent my time running in and out of the windy entrances. (The logic, as it was explained to me then, is that radiation doesn't go around corners.) In hindsight, it all made as much sense as the "duck and tuck" drills we did in school as we crouched under our desks to protect ourselves from the exploding bombs.

But while I was playing in the bomb shelter, a woman came up to me and asked me how I would like to live in one of these. I looked around and gave the only sensible answer. To this, the woman replied, "Then tell your parents to write the president to get him to stop this madness." I remember thinking this lady was a bit strange. But the point she made has always stuck with me as a reminder of how close we actually came—in my lifetime—to nuclear war.

Was Kennedy's behavior during the Cuban missile crisis personal or geopolitical? The answer is both. It may have had personal roots, but at that point there was probably very little geopolitical alternative to the confrontation if the global balance of power was to be maintained. The same could be said of Iraq. President George W. Bush doubtless also had a visceral reaction to his opponent of the day, Saddam Hussein, as did many of his advisers. The man had tried to assassinate his father after all. What son wouldn't feel strongly? Moreover, the decision not to topple Saddam in 1991 had led to nothing but frustration for America, as President Bill Clinton could attest. Saddam had taken our decision not to depose him as a sign of weakness, brutally attacking those who threatened his regime.

There were also very solid geopolitical reasons to pick Iraq from the list of rogue nations that threatened the United States and the whole world order. Chief among these was that in no other case had diplomatic actions been so exhausted. There had been sixteen failed UN resolutions calling for Saddam to comply with international law, and the oil-for-food embargo program was clearly broken. Most shockingly, money from the oil-for-food program was being diverted to Saddam Hussein's regime, providing him with the foreign exchange to circumvent sanctions and buy what he wanted on international markets. The U.S. General Accountability Office estimated that his regime generated $10 billion in illegal revenue. If international law was to ever have any role in mediating conflicts between states, the status quo could not stand. The members of the Security Council knew that when they passed their resolution threatening "serious consequences" for Iraqi noncompliance with their resolutions in the fall of 2002.

Even though Saddam's collection of weapons of mass destruction was limited to some missiles with a range that could potentially strike Israel and were in violation of his international agreements, it is plain that given free rein he likely would have reconstituted his nuclear program by now, given the nuclear push being made by Shia clerics in Iran. Extensive documents seized after the 1991 Gulf War from captured Iraqi government files show that his nuclear program was much further advanced than was thought at the time. In the wake of 9/11, it was a legitimate position, though not necessarily the only possible one, that a president should err on the side of geopolitical caution when it came to taking a risk of a rogue regime having weapons of mass destruction.

But the obvious conflict between the personal and the geopolitical created a big problem with Bush going to war. In retrospect, critics can claim that the reasons must have been purely personal since the threat from weapons of mass destruction was far from imminent. And it is a well-established point of legal logic that one cannot prove a negative, so there is no way for Bush to establish that this was not the case. Moreover, history never allows us to run a counterfactual. What would have happened had we not invaded Iraq? Would life in the Middle East have gone on happily ever after? The right basis to contrast what happened in Iraq is certainly not some hypothetical "Peace in Our Time." So, in the near term, regardless of what the actual facts of Iraq may be or may have been, the rules of evidence in the court of public opinion are stacked against Bush.

But the verdict of history would have gone against Kennedy as well—in an even more decisive way—had his gambit in the Cuban missile crisis not have succeeded. We will never be able to fully prevent our leaders from making emotional decisions—they are men and women just like us even when they walk in the shoes of the presidency. Nor is it likely that we would be happy with a president utterly lacking in emotion in making decisions. In fact, one of the criteria that pollsters try to ascertain in assessing the public's views is whether a presidential candidate "understands the problems of people like you." But we can and should expect our presidents to gather facts and ask hard questions before they make the biggest decision of their term in office. And that is the purpose of the next memo.

FROM: LAWRENCE B. LINDSEY
SUBJECT: GOING TO WAR CHECKLIST
January 20, 2009

The previous memo laid out the case against going to war and the high cost to you, both personally and politically, to make the decision. Still, there are times when there is no alternative. You may be president during one of those times. You are the only person who can determine that. This is a checklist to help you ask the right questions before the war starts.

IS WAR INEVITABLE?

Stated differently and in a historic context, you must decide whether peaceful interactions with the enemy will turn out to be merely appeasement or lasting peace. This requires you to place yourself in our enemy's position, not just by saying, "If I were him," but by adopting his values and worldview. You can't simply make our enemy a mirror image of yourself because his frame of reference may be quite different.

For example, Osama bin Laden's view of Afghanistan is quite different from ours. We see the ejection of the Soviet Union as a victory in the Cold War. He sees it as a victory in Islam's holy war to spread its faith worldwide. In a CNN interview in 1997, bin Laden said that "the myth of the superpower was destroyed not only in my mind but also in the minds of all Muslims" because of the Soviet defeat in Afghanistan by the mujahideen. Nor is he likely to stop there, and in fact he is quite confident about his ultimate ability to triumph. "The Russian soldier is more courageous and patient than the U.S. soldier," he told London's Arab newspaper *al-Quds al-Arabi* in 1996. "Our battle with the United States is easy compared with the battles in which we engaged in Afghanistan."[4] Or consider President Mahmoud

Ahmadinejad of Iran: "Just as the Soviet Union was wiped out and today does not exist, so will the Zionist regime soon be wiped out."[5]

There is quite possibly an important historic parallel here. Prime Minister Neville Chamberlain of Great Britain and Prime Minister Edouard Daladier of France had a worldview shaped by the horrors of World War I that convinced them that another such war in Europe was unthinkable. They assumed that anyone would reach the same conclusion. Adolf Hitler's view was also shaped by World War I, but his view was that it was a German defeat that had to be revenged by a subsequent German victory. This view was further perverted by the notion that the Germans were genetically superior and thus also *deserved* to rule the rest of Europe and would have had they not been "sold out." Chamberlain genuinely thought that Hitler was a man with whom he could do business and hence made a deal with him at Munich. Chamberlain was wrong.

America is a safe superpower precisely because we have the built-in institutional constraints against going to war previously discussed. One of those constraints is that we believe that *others have the same constraints*. That is not necessarily so. Nor is it the case that seemingly hideous regimes do not share our view. The Soviet Union is a case in point. Stalin, for example, probably did not share our perceptions of the horrors of war, though he did have a deep fear of defeat. After his death, Khrushchev's 1956 speech to the twentieth party congress made it clear that the dominant part of the ruling elite desired a more constrained and less personality-driven leadership. The Soviet Union became a country with which one was more likely to be able to do business. The same thing could happen in Iran. And, in fact, we are in a peaceful coexistence mode with Osama bin Laden's home country, Saudi Arabia, a nation the government of which he seeks to overthrow.

Again, only you can make this determination on behalf of the country. Your determination will be a personal one, not a bureaucratic one, and it may be driven by forces outside your control. The British foreign policy bureaucracy at Whitehall that served and advised

Chamberlain also advised Winston Churchill. British intelligence about Hitler's intentions did not change; instead, the prevailing judgment was proven decidedly wrong by events. Nor was the British decision a military one. What changed was the personal worldview of the leader. Therefore, your worldview should be an informed one and one that is exposed to a variety of thinking on the subject.

RECOMMENDATION: Your judgment about whether war is avoidable should be informed by a variety of knowledgeable people throughout the government, business, and academia. You should aggressively seek out a wide variety of thinkers and analysts and require your staff to find such people, not just those who either support your view or support the consensus view of the American foreign policy establishment. Then make up your mind.

IS THE WAR WINNABLE?

This is not just a military subject. Andrew Roberts, author of *A History of the English Speaking Peoples since 1900*, argues that a nation's will to win is at least as important as its fighting capacity.[6] This involves a variety of social and economic as well as military factors. Again, this is a strategic judgment that only you can make.

The military component of this decision is likely to follow a predictable pattern. The military hierarchy is unlikely to tell the commander in chief that a given war is militarily unwinnable. Rather, they will provide a laundry list of the resources they will need to win the war. Being appropriately risk averse, the laundry list will doubtless be more than what is *most likely* to be needed. Undisturbed by civilian oversight, the military's perception of its requirements will approach a "worst-case" scenario. They have every interest in making sure that they do not fail and a strong bureaucratic interest in making sure they do not have to come back to you for more.

The initial military request is also likely to exceed what you can prudently deliver, weighing all the other concerns that you face. You will doubtless have to push back and say, "Do you *really* need ..." But there is a habit in this paring back the "wish list" that began in the 1960s with Secretary of Defense Robert McNamara and that has proceeded to the current day that determining military needs is like a linear programming model in managing civilian production. It is not, and a variety of American military adventures have proven this. The men and women who will go into harm's way need to know that they will have every conceivable resource to support their effort. This is not a mathematical concept; it is one of leadership.

RECOMMENDATION: While the Pentagon cannot be given everything it wants, you should assume that their requests are an indication of what a worst-case scenario might involve. You should prepare to meet those requirements as much as possible.

A part of the military recommendation on "winnability" involves the Doctrine of Overwhelming Force—the so-called Powell Doctrine again. But the use of overwhelming force runs into one of the key social questions that you must answer: **Can you really use overwhelming force if your enemy isn't the people of the country you are about to fight but its government? Again, this is an issue that only you will be able to decide**.

America's ethical traditions do tend to run against the notion of harming "innocent" people. But this has been waived when it was decided that the key to victory was breaking the will of the enemy to fight. General William Tecumseh Sherman's march through Georgia was one such example and was sanctioned by President Abraham Lincoln, who, incidentally, benefited politically as a result. The firebombings of Dresden and Tokyo, not to mention the atomic bombing of Hiroshima and Nagasaki, were examples of this. Hiroshima and Nagasaki are often defended ethically as having saved both Japanese and American lives by ending the war sooner and thus obviating the need for an invasion of Japan.

But the pendulum does seem to have swung in the opposite direction today. In part this is probably due to global news coverage that brings images of human suffering and carnage into our homes. In Iraq, for example, the military showed footage of its efforts to minimize collateral damage, even blowing up an Iraqi tank under a bridge with a smart bomb while leaving the bridge intact. Moreover, our effort in Iraq was to liberate the people from a tyrant who used poison gas even on his own population. It would have been impossible to portray the war as being against the whole Iraqi nation. This undermines the possibility of doing "whatever it takes" to win.

But if you are not willing to do whatever it takes to win, by definition, your chances of winning are reduced. You are making the value judgment that you would rather lose the war than, say, cause some level of civilian casualties. The answer of your military advisers is likely to be that they can, in fact, still win the war, but it will take even more resources since the rules of engagement will prescribe the use of those resources that are available. **Most important, it will take far longer to win the war since the will to fight of those who oppose us will not be decisively broken**. This will entail a long and messy policing operation at a minimum.

A second aspect of this issue has to do with a widening of the war. One aspect of the "innocent people" problem is that noncombatant nations might get drawn in. The most contentious example of this occurred in the Korean War, when General Douglas MacArthur did not follow orders regarding the rules of engagement and took his troops too close to the Yalu River. MacArthur's action brought China into the conflict, but MacArthur's argument was that the war was unwinnable unless he did this. President Harry Truman was eventually forced to fire MacArthur for being insubordinate and advocating a direct war with China. A political firestorm ensued within America as supporters of MacArthur argued that Truman wasn't letting the military do its job.

The reverse political firestorm followed President Richard Nixon's decision to invade Cambodia, an action that the president's military advisers felt was necessary to stop the resupply of the enemy from just across the border. Many argued that Nixon exceeded his presidential authority, and concealing information about the Cambodia invasion was one of the articles of impeachment brought against Nixon, although it was ultimately rejected.

RECOMMENDATION: The rules of engagement are inseparable from the war's winnability, and there is no point in engaging in a war unless you are prepared to win. Determine how far you might ultimately be willing to go—not how far you would prefer to have to go—and be prepared to pay the consequences. Then ask your military advisers what resources they will need.

WHAT DO YOU DO AFTER YOU WIN THE WAR?

One often hears the phrase about Iraq, "We won the war but lost the peace." To be precise, *you* will ultimately determine—and will be held fully responsible for—whether we lost the peace in Iraq. It is certainly accurate to criticize your predecessor for not having been adequately prepared for the huge problems that followed a very rapid and successful war to depose Saddam. Although the criticism is accurate, he is far from the first president to fall short in this regard.

The reason for this failing is that discussing what to do after a war is won before the war is fought is often viewed as a political nonstarter. First, it smacks of hubris, and a recurring recommendation from history is to prepare for the worst case and not assume an easy victory. Second, the discussion is seen as politically divisive and may undermine the war effort from the start.

Start with President Lincoln and the Civil War. Lincoln's decision to go for a generous peace of "with malice toward none, with charity for all" was decidedly unpopular. Lincoln himself did not enunciate that proposal until his second inaugural, less than two months before the war was actually won. Obviously, his assassination complicated the political process, but the generous conduct of Reconstruction was the root cause of the impeachment of his successor, Andrew Johnson. The congressional elections of 1866 produced a landslide win for the Radical Republicans, who sought to impose a punitive postwar policy on the South, the very opposite of what Lincoln had proposed. History later showed that Lincoln had the better approach, but had he raised the idea of a generous peace earlier, he doubtless would have encountered political problems he didn't need during the war.

President Woodrow Wilson was also an advocate of a fairly generous peace and was particularly focused on creating an institutional framework for avoiding a second conflict: the League of Nations. Instead, the victorious allies produced a rather punitive peace with unpayable demands for reparations on Germany that was a root cause of World War II. At home, Wilson's plan for entry into the League of Nations was defeated in the Senate despite a nationwide whistle-stop campaign for it by Wilson. Again, the case for a more generous peace was certainly borne out by history, a point made most persuasively by John Maynard Keynes in his tome *The Economic Consequences of the Peace*.[7] But Wilson did not and could not effectively have fought that battle before the peace was achieved.

President Franklin Roosevelt's own administration was torn on the subject of Germany. Near the end of the war, the dominant faction, led by Treasury Secretary Henry Morganthau, proposed a punitive peace in which Germany would be dissolved into much smaller independent states, deprived of heavy industry, and returned to an agrarian basis. Both Roosevelt and Churchill had approved this plan at the Second Quebec Conference in 1944. There is a lot of evidence that one of the key architects of the plan, Deputy Secretary Harry Dexter White, was a Soviet agent, and it is certainly clear that the Soviet Union would have benefited from such an approach. In any event, the plan was never implemented, although a good many of General Dwight Eisenhower's staff were borrowed from the Treasury Department and did take a very heavy hand in creating policies that would limit German economic growth. The German economic miracle followed a policy coup on June 20, 1948, by the occupation government's finance minister, Ludwig Erhard, who illegally abolished price controls, cut taxes, and engineered a currency reform by decree. Erhard admits he did it on a Sunday because the American military staff didn't work on Sundays and so wouldn't be around to stop him. The widespread lines for basic commodities disappeared almost instantaneously, and the

American occupation authorities felt it would be imprudent to roll back Erhard's reforms. Needless to say, this is hardly a resounding endorsement of American planning for the postwar situation.

The evidence suggests three recurring themes. First, the immediate postwar situation is always chaotic and entailed virtually no preparation. Living conditions in the occupied areas are always bleak for a minimum of two to three years after a victory, and the military is unprepared to deal with this. Second, a generous peace is difficult to advance politically in large part because it appears to benefit an *enemy* who was just recently trying to kill us. This was particularly true when the enemy was the country at large, not just the government. Third, in the long run, preparing for a generous peace advances America's long-term interests.

RECOMMENDATION: Quietly but thoroughly prepare the mechanisms for a generous postwar administration. It may be politically and morally easier to implement such a plan if it follows a victory that is quick and decisive and that involves a minimum number of constraints on wartime military activity.

DO YOU HAVE AN EXIT STRATEGY?

America must be the only superpower in history that debates this issue at the earliest stages of its entry into any recent conflict. Certainly, Rome never considered how it was going to evacuate from Gaul or Britain as it marched in to conquer these lands. Britain and France did not plan the dissolution of their empires when they were building them. The Soviet Empire certainly never contemplated retreat. America is different in this regard because it never actually plans to stay, though sometimes it does.

Interestingly, we tend to stay when we are most successful. World War II was one of America's most successful wars. Two leading world powers, Germany and Japan, who were considered hopelessly belligerent and authoritarian cultures, became models of peaceful democracy. Of course, American troops are still stationed in both countries six decades after the end of hostilities. While American taxpayers may have occasionally expressed resentment over this, this is not the kind of nonexit about which you should be primarily concerned.

The need for an exit strategy is crucial when things do not go well. Technically, this should not be an issue if you have made it this far down this chapter's checklist. First, if there really was no alternative to war, then losing a war is not an option. Second, if you had prepared both the public and the military for the struggle that lay ahead, then the world's dominant superpower should not be in the position of not achieving its objectives. But things go wrong. Plan for it.

Britain faced this problem when France collapsed in May 1940 and the British forces withdrew to Dunkirk for evacuation to Britain. Ultimately, Churchill mobilized all boats in Britain, including private fishing boats and yachts, to pull off a successful evacuation, an act that may have saved Britain. Suffice it to say that the collapse of France was something that was not supposed to happen.

America faced this in the Philippines in World War II when Roosevelt faced the choice of allocating the fleet to the Battle of the North Atlantic or evacuating the troops from Bataan and chose the North Atlantic. In Vietnam, America was forced into a humiliating evacuation by helicopter from the roof of its embassy after Congress had cut off funding for the South Vietnamese government, resulting in its collapse. Again, the Paris peace talks did not contemplate this outcome. Churchill and MacArthur vowed to return, in a war where the alternative to ultimate victory was unthinkable. Americans returned to Vietnam only as investors a quarter century later.

But even if withdrawal is done in an honorable fashion in the short run, the consequences may be horrific in the longer term. The British withdrawal from India and Pakistan on their independence resulted in the deaths of as many as a million people and the forcible relocation of 10 million people. The French withdrawal from Algeria created substantial disruptions. Should you ultimately choose to withdraw from Iraq, the chances of a bloodbath seem high. There are cases where America did ultimately withdraw without chaos, the Philippines being one such example. But the sad fact is that the dominant model is either a semipermanent American presence or a problematic American withdrawal. You need to be prepared for either.

RECOMMENDATION: Before embarking on a war, you must have preparations for both a long commitment and a premature retreat.

HOW WILL YOU FINANCE THE WAR?

There is a widely held but utterly false belief that wars are good for the economy. Taking resources that could be used to build homes, manufacture appliances, or invent and develop new technologies and using them to make things that get blown up is not good for an economy. The only thing worse economically is losing a war, which in the process means having your existing stock of homes, appliances, and technologies destroyed by a foreign power or terrorist attack. A wise nation goes to war not to build a new economy but to protect what it has.

Because of this, the benefits of a successful war designed to protect what you have are enjoyed for many years in the future. Had our wars not been fought or had they not been successful, generations of Americans would have been poorer for the failure. As a result, there is an equitable ground to spread the costs of war over a period of time. This is the implicit reason in political theory why there is little objection to deficit spending in wartime. Should you go to war, there is little doubt that you too will be using deficit finance for a portion of the expenses.

But that does not mean that your entire war effort needs to be deficit financed. You are diverting current resources toward the war effort. Very large-scale deficit financing tends to shift funds that would have gone into home construction, the purchases of durable goods like cars, and business investment into war finance. There is little reason why current spending by both the public and the private sector should not be curtailed as well to offset part of the war cost.

Taxes were raised by President Franklin Roosevelt during World War II, and the withholding of the current year's taxes was introduced.

But Roosevelt also cut a number of his cherished New Deal domestic spending priorities as well. Between 1939 and 1944, nondefense spending fell by 37 percent. President Harry Truman did something similar in the Korean War, slashing nondefense spending by 25 percent in just one year, between 1950 and 1951.

Financing a portion of the war effort through a reduction in domestic spending, and if absolutely necessary higher taxes, serves an indirect purpose as well: it involves the public at large in sacrifice for the war. During World War II, other techniques were also used to convey the sense that the public at large was doing its part: scrap metal drives, air warden volunteers, and rationing of certain goods like gasoline and chocolate. As a practical matter, few of these efforts would pass a strict cost–benefit test of effectiveness. They were doubtless costly to administer and produced little direct benefit. But the feeling of the time was that this sort of sacrifice built support for the war because individuals, through their sacrifice, were implicitly buying into the effort.

A similar argument could be made about the military draft. Economists have long argued that a military draft is an inefficient means of providing the manpower for war. Instead, economists generally recommend paying troops a reasonable rate of pay and providing other, nonmaterial forms of support as well in order to encourage volunteers. In World War II, the manpower needs probably required the conscription of all or most of the physically able population of young males, and a market-clearing price was probably not feasible. The same could not be said of the Cold War, even though a military draft was maintained. Instead, that draft was used largely as a budget-saving device. A key point is made about the notion of the "shared sacrifice" case for using a draft. While a World War II type of situation in which manpower needs are so dramatic that conscription is almost mandatory does represent a way of sharing the sacrifice, the Cold War draft actually produced the opposite result. Instead of sharing the sacrifice, conscription allowed an artificially low cost of military spending and thus reduced the need to raise taxes or cut other programs. This concentrated the cost of defense among those who were forced to serve and limited the sacrifices made by the general population: either taxpayers or recipients of government services. In normal circumstances, a volunteer army that is adequately paid both monetarily and in the respect of the citizenry involves a more equitable sharing of the sacrifices of defense than does a draft.

The final source of war finance is inflation. To some extent, inflationary pressures are inevitable in a wartime situation. Resources devoted to normal civilian use are being reallocated to defense. This puts upward pressure on their price, other things equal. Labor markets are tighter because more individuals are employed either by being in uniform or by substituting for those who are in uniform who would otherwise be in civilian occupations. But ultimately, inflation can be sustained only by monetary policy. Central banks tend to cause inflation in wartime because they purchase some of the war-financing bonds issued by the government, increasing the money supply and thereby driving up the amount of money chasing the available supply of goods.

Governments often try to mask this by putting on price controls and instituting rationing programs. There is little evidence that these efforts succeed in doing anything other than creating a black market and thereby lowering respect for the sacrifices being made to fight a war. They should be avoided. If inflation is to be avoided, the better call for you to make is to the chairman of the Federal Reserve, not to some war allocation board. But do not fear a little inflation if the cause is worth it. In the short run, it can be a form of indirect tax on existing holders of financial wealth.

The key component of planning war financing is getting a realistic cost estimate. There are many institutional reasons that you might get bad information, especially if the Defense Department wants war. That is why it is so important to ask for the worst-case scenario and not just a central tendency. The worst-case scenario will also give you one more opportunity to rethink your desire to go to war.

RECOMMENDATION: The traditional means of government financing its activities are needed in wartime as well: cutting nondefense spending and, if necessary, raising taxes. This means you will be sacrificing coveted programs not related to the war. In more extreme situations, deficit spending, inflation, and nontraditional means of finance, including conscription, can also be used with decreasing amounts of efficiency.

ARE YOU GETTING GOOD INFORMATION?

Each of the items on this checklist has placed you in the position of having to make a decision on the basis of a broad set of information, not just military matters. You will need individuals with a deep knowledge of the country and region you are going to war with, knowledge of economics, social policy, and possibly cultural and religious issues. The government does not have a monopoly on such people, and, in particular, the existing foreign affairs bureaucracies may not even have the best and the brightest in these areas.

The decision-making apparatus that you have set up is not inclined to be broadly inclusive. Membership in the National Security Council is limited, for example. There is, of course, a natural desire to preserve secrecy and the confidentiality of the decision-making process, especially during wartime. Hence, these meetings tend to be quite exclusive. But the price of that can be to cut you off from some of the country's best minds and from valuable information.

You must develop a means of reaching out—both within your government, to the private sector, and to the opposition—to discover people who have information to share. These include both the business community, academics, and think-tank scholars. Even more counterintuitive is that some of the best information about the country you may be contemplating going to war with may be held by individuals in the fourth estate—the dreaded press! Some may have served assignments in sensitive regions or have other direct knowledge. In days gone by, when the country was more unified about its foreign policy priorities, presidents would not hesitate to ask for help from any American.

RECOMMENDATION: Information and intelligence is one of the most valuable weapons any country can have in wartime. Do not cut off these possible sources should you take this nation to war. Even better, do your best to re-create the old days when the media and the president worked together. Before going to war, call in the heads of the major news networks to personally and privately brief them on the unsolvable nature of the problem and unified national response that is needed to prevail. In this age of skepticism, only the president can do this.

FIVE

✦✦✦

ARE WE READY FOR ANOTHER DARK DAY?

IT WAS A CRYSTAL-CLEAR September morning, the kind that Washingtonians really relish after the sweltering heat, hazy skies, and humidity of August. All the kids were back in school, another reason to be thankful. Markets had been having a rough ride. The collapse of the NASDAQ bubble had spilled over into the general economy and blue-chip stocks as well. So, as usual, CNBC was on with the sound off, the graphics flashing across the screen providing the continuous update of financial information.

The staff of the National Economic Council (NEC) was gathered around the conference table in my paneled office on the second floor of the West Wing, physically just above the cabinet room. It was a daily ritual. Information in the White House is a two-way flow that begins with the senior staff meeting in the Roosevelt Room at 7:30. There, with the assistants to the president gathered around the table, the news of what was happening in Congress, the media, and the country at large was shared, and an outline of the administration's reaction to it took shape. This cascade of information was then passed on to the deputy assistants and special assistants in individual staff meetings in each of the various divisions of the White House bureaucracy. The NEC staff meeting was one of these and started at 8:30.

It was my favorite time of day, and, frankly, although I enjoyed working at the White House, it is the only part of the experience that I can say without any reservation that I truly miss. The reason was the quality of the staff, most of them in their thirties at the time. Today, when we gather at social events, the greetings are half-joking formalities of "Mr. Secretary" or "Mr. Chairman" and some good-natured ribbing about the seven-figure salaries that those who have already left government can command for their talents.

Each of these individuals was in charge of a policy area such as energy, trade, technology, health care, or financial markets. The purpose of this meeting was to learn what was happening on the front lines of their policy areas and give guidance on how to advance the priorities of the administration. Each policy area had but a few minutes of rather intensive exchange. But then every one of these talented individuals could go forward with an almost completely free hand to organize interagency meetings, talk to business leaders or lobbyists, or exchange views with senior staff on the Hill and have my complete trust. It was great that they were young because they were full of the energy and enthusiasm needed to put in the long and grueling day their job demanded. This management style was one I had learned a dozen years earlier when I was one of them, long before I became gray and, well, decidedly middle aged.

One of these staffers, now a partner in one of the world's leading hedge funds, asked to go first since he had to leave the meeting early to get to another meeting across the street. He delivered his morning update and ducked out. A minute later he popped back in and interrupted the meeting to announce that a plane had just struck the World Trade Center. He had worked in financial markets before and had an ear for detecting impending trouble. At that point we still weren't sure if this was intentional or just an accident. After all, a B-25 bomber had once flown into the Empire State Building during World War II. But given the World Trade Center's location near the Stock Exchange and the Federal Reserve Bank of New York, we knew it would be a challenging and unprecedented day.

Seventeen minutes later, after most of my staff had just returned to the Eisenhower Executive Office Building, the second plane hit, removing all doubt about the intentional nature of the act. What we didn't know then was that we had been and still were a target, sitting just twenty feet from the edge of the Oval Office. The next thing I remember was the Secret Service going down the floor asking us to move to the Mess, which is halfway between the ground floor and the basement.

I was never one to automatically follow instructions. But, having seen what happened to the World Trade Center, a building with several thousand times the mass of the White House, I didn't think that moving to the ground floor gave me a particularly higher probability of survival. Instead, I picked up the phone and called my wife. If I was to have time for one last conversation, I was going to avail myself of the opportunity. I told her that we were at war and that I had no idea when I'd be home but that she should take care of the kids and I would find them all somehow. Six years later it sounds a bit dramatic, but it sure didn't seem that way at the time. The conversation ended with an impatient Secret Service agent coming into my office, saying in the firmest tone that I knew I wasn't permitted to ignore, "Sir, go to the Mess."

By the time I got there, the futility of seeking shelter in the Mess had become apparent even to the Secret Service. They ordered us outside, where other agents were shouting, "Run, run, run, incoming plane." Run where? No one had a clue. Instinct suggested that it would be wise to put a building between ourselves and the White House. But, again, I will always be grateful to those men and women passengers who sacrificed themselves in Pennsylvania so that the laws of physics that applied when an airplane hits a building a block from where I was standing were not put to the test.

We moved from the street to the nearby Chrysler government relations office, where the husband of one of the people on our staff worked. An hour later the Secret Service found me and escorted me through streets patrolled by soldiers holding submachine guns to the bunker under the East Wing of the White House, where I joined Vice President Dick Cheney, members of the cabinet, and some of the other White House senior staff. President Franklin Roosevelt's stated preference for being on the White House lawn "enjoying the fireworks" rather than in the bomb shelter became quite understandable. It was decidedly claustrophobic, and the air circulation was inadequate. The Secret Service was maintaining space around the vice president so he could get some air.

The chaos of the day belied the fact that there actually was in place, somewhere in some three-ring binder on a shelf in some office, an orderly plan for what everyone was supposed to do in the event of an emergency. On the back of my White House security badge were the letters "ES," which I now know stood for something like "Evacuated Staff." If the White House was under attack and the president was to be evacuated by helicopter, I was supposed to make my way down to the South Lawn to be evacuated with him. He wasn't in town that day, so the orders then got fuzzy. The most logical would be to find the vice president and stay with him. Trouble was, I usually had no idea where the vice president was, and I doubtless wouldn't on any other day in which the White House was under attack. But that was the least of it.

My biggest problem on September 11 was that no one had briefed me about what ES meant (there's a lot of things on a security badge), and the Secret Service agents who told me first to go to the mess and then to run, run, run, didn't know what they were supposed to do with me either. This deficiency has now been remedied, I understand. But there were other flaws in this plan. For example, if the White House were actually under attack from the air, I doubt evacuation by helicopter would have been such a good idea either. Several weeks later the people who plan for these things provided us with chemical and biological warfare (CBW) gear and training on how to use it, so that box has been checked, but there was some debate on how I was going to hang my badge with the ES on it on the outside of the CBW outfit.

Herein lies a lesson. No one can write detailed orders for every eventuality because even the largest and most creative group of thinkers can't think of every possible emergency. Hijacking planes and crashing them into buildings wasn't something that had been widely anticipated. So in my opinion, one of the big lessons of September 11 and its immediate aftermath is that in a crisis, there is no substitute for creative thinking. Creative thinking cannot be put into a three-ring binder. It is like the received wisdom of the military: no plan of battle survives the first shot.

Instead, the bureaucratic impulse is to create redundancy so that "someone is always in charge." This is called "continuity of government." The two essentials of continuity are redundancy and hierarchy. You need multiple layers of backup, but with multiple layers you need a hierarchy of command so that one and only one layer is in charge at any one time. At least, that is how it works in theory.

In practice, the ES on the back of my badge got me in a CBW suit and gas mask and onto a helicopter with the president if he was in town. The lower-level staff were supposed to disperse and return to their homes to wait for instructions. My deputy at the White House and my colleague in assembling this book had the privilege of staying at the White House if we were under attack and was to be in charge if the helicopter went down, assuming he survived. Talk about drawing the short straw.

Even if the formal plans for continuity in government don't work out perfectly (and they won't), there are a number of intangible factors that will kick in that really can't be planned for. One of the most important is the indomitable spirit of the people who serve in government. The median age of the nineteen people on my staff was mid-thirties. At forty-eight, I was definitely old enough to be the father of many. As they went outside that day after having been evacuated with the order "Run, run, run, incoming plane," they could see the smoke rising from the Pentagon just across the river. At 9:45 that morning, they ran for the gates and generally kept going. Some walked for miles until they reached home or another safe haven.

Few of these people had ever felt their lives were actually in danger before that day. But by the end of that day, many who had experienced a real fear of death for the first time just hours before were clamoring to get back into the building. Anyone would have been forgiven for not showing up at staff meeting the next morning, but almost everyone did. We all knew we were at war and that if we were afraid to come to work in a building that may as well have had a bull's-eye painted on the roof, then our enemies had already won. Fear was replaced by a sense of duty without anyone giving an order. It was an automatic response. It was a great privilege in the days that followed to work with this team. In its own way, it was also therapeutic.

But that tone was also set by the commander in chief and his decision to return to the White House. He didn't just have to overcome his fear that day. He had to override the Secret Service and others on his staff who urged him to go to a safe place. In so doing, he doubtless also overrode the bureaucratic manual on continuity in government. His return to join the vice president, much of his cabinet, and his senior staff was the antithesis of redundancy. It was a sign of unity and a sign of resolve. It was a signal to the country that the president was where he belonged, prepared to command, and not hiding in a bunker somewhere. It was an act much like King George VI and the royal family's staying at Buckingham Palace during the London Blitz, with the Royal Standard flying full. President George W. Bush has endured many criticisms of his presidency in the ensuing years. But his performance and courage that evening and in the weeks that followed were exemplary.

That night I remember taking a deep breath when I was let out of the bunker and allowed to breathe fresh air again. I was proba-

bly one of the first cars allowed to leave the parking lot on West
Executive Avenue, around 11:00 that night, and it being a convert-
ible, I left the roof down the entire trip enjoying the pleasant night
air. I was grateful for the air. It cleared my head and allowed me to
think about what would happen next. I was also grateful for the
freedom that puts its trust in people to do the right thing.

This sentiment is not universal, and it is interesting how recollections of the day differ. One staffer at the National Security Council later wrote that he went home late that night but returned,
packing a revolver, to a White House nearly empty with the parking lot deserted. But the Secret Service had not allowed people to
drive home after the evacuation, so people who had left before me
and those who had not returned after the initial evacuation still had
their cars on West Executive Avenue. I am also not sure whom this
staffer intended to shoot with his revolver at the White House. The
terrorist attacks of that day had been staged by crashing airplanes
into buildings, not launching commando raids. But, though he was
a key witness before the 9/11 Commission, his recollections of that
day are quite different from mine and those of many others.

This man's response to 9/11 was fairly rare among the White
House staff. He attempted to use the event as a way of gaining
bureaucratic power. He circulated a draft executive order for the
president that contained a provision delegating to himself the president's wartime authorities to take control of the communications
infrastructure, including the Internet, during a crisis. He also tried
to give himself the same title as Karl Rove. It was just one document in a period of massive organization change, but one of my
staffers caught it and lined up other agencies to join us in trying to
block his efforts. Later he attacked the NEC, the Office of Management and Budget, and the Office of Science and Technology
Policy as being part of an Axis of Evil for blocking his power grab.

More understandable in the weeks that followed were the
efforts of some people to advance arguably well-intentioned ideas
that addressed a limited part of the terrorism threat but had not

thought through unintended consequences. On the lighter side, one of these ideas was to ban drinking on airplanes. The incident occurred in the Roosevelt Room just before a meeting with the president to find a way of getting the airline industry, which had been grounded on 9/11, flying again.

The meeting was going to be a tough one for me. Most of my colleagues were against the idea of a bailout to get the planes flying. I reasoned that it was going to be tough to resume air travel on a commercially viable basis not only because the industry was flat broke from having been grounded but also because of the not unreasonable fear that 9/11 had left about flying. When I heard this line about banning drinking on board by one of the more socially conservative members of the administration before the meeting started, I had to retort that I thought that free drinks for everyone on the plane was a much better approach to the problem.

Some of the issues that came up in the weeks that followed were far more serious, particularly the response to a smallpox attack. When one contemplates all the ways mankind could decimate the population and destroy civilization as we know it, reintroducing smallpox into the population has to be among the most horrific. It is one of our species' greatest successes that we have eliminated this plague from the entire human population. But strains of the disease still exist in laboratories in at least a few countries.

At an interagency briefing on the subject, the plan of the military and public health officials was to quarantine affected areas, effectively banning the movement of people between metropolitan areas. When I asked how they were going to prevent the roughly 900,000 business travelers who were away from their families on any given day from returning home, the effective answer was "forcibly if necessary." Then I inquired who was going to be at the supermarkets to prevent food riots. After all, nearly all the produce in the country that we consume every day is moved by truck between metropolitan areas. There was no response.

The challenge posed to our country by terrorists is a real one. It is certainly necessary to plan responses in advance, where possible. But my experience with the process of actually carrying this out has me worried about the answers that government may actually come up with. Bureaucracy is by its nature divided into separate silos. Each particular group is assigned a given mission to solve a particular problem. The danger is that the particular silo focuses on a limited part of the problem, ignoring the unintended consequences of its actions on other parts of society. That was as true with the National Security Council staffer's plan to take control of the Internet as it was with banning drinks on airplanes or quarantining the population when there was smallpox.

But I am getting ahead of myself. I discuss that very issue in the next memorandum to the president.

MEMORANDUM FOR THE PRESIDENT

FROM: LAWRENCE B. LINDSEY
SUBJECT: THE AFTERMATH OF A TERRORIST ATTACK
January 20, 2009

Seven years after 9/11, it is still hard for me to write about the events of that day without stirring some deep emotions. Although we have been spared a repetition of that nightmare in the intervening years, the odds are still high enough that there will be a similar event during your tenure that this memo is included to give you a guidepost to what will happen in the days and weeks after.

One of the problems in thinking this issue through is appearing to be overly analytic, even clinical, about events that involve the deaths of hundreds or thousands of people. As president, you will have to bifurcate your emotional state, *because your job will demand it*, between the openly empathic and the coldly analytical. When you visit the victims and hug their families, you will no doubt feel and must show genuine emotion. But when you return to the White House, you will have to evaluate the risks facing the nation in a manner in which the tears on the faces you have just seen blur into cold, hard facts.

THE THREAT AND THE RESPONSE

The place to start is to realize that the intent of the terrorists was not to kill the particular victims whose families you have just seen. It is to destroy our country and our way of life. It is easy to have an emotional response to the murders the terrorists committed that involves a crackdown on our most essential civil liberties. It is easy to resolve that this should never happen again and place restrictions on the transportation of people and goods and financial flows that wreak havoc on our economy. But, if you do so, you will have achieved the terrorists' objectives. You—and not they—will have destroyed our way of life by your response to their action.

The first call I received the morning of September 12, 2001, was from the auto industry. They told me that they were about to shut down auto production in Michigan. It had been a short night, much of it spent contemplating the economic fallout from the events of the previous day, but I was surprised and said so. The response was that the "just-in-time" inventory system allowed them eleven hours of parts with which to build cars. Many of those parts crossed the Ambassador Bridge from Windsor, Ontario, to Detroit. We had tightened border restrictions overnight, and the parts were not coming through. Treasury Secretary Paul O'Neill and I spent much of the morning getting to the bottom of the problem and finding a way for auto parts to continue flowing across the border through special lanes.

It was but one of dozens of the pieces of economic fallout from 9/11 that we dealt with in the weeks after the attack. Detroit is 500 miles from the Pentagon and 600 miles from Manhattan and was unaffected by the terrorist attack. It was dramatically affected by our response. This is not to say that our response was inappropriate, but it did not represent a sustainable situation for the economy. Similarly, there was no acceptable alternative to grounding all airplanes on 9/11. But leaving them grounded too long would have destroyed our economy and a good part of our freedom to travel.

It is impressive how well our economy recovered after 9/11. It is also impressive how our essential liberties were preserved. We have unfettered freedom of speech and of the press. Religious liberty was unaffected, even though one aspect of the terrorists' motives was religious. The rights to bear arms, to a jury trial, and to be secure in our persons and possessions are all still intact. We have had four national elections, including the one that you just won, in which campaigning was unhampered by legal responses to the terrorist attack.

Today, we take all this for granted, but this happy outcome was far from ensured on 9/11. It will be your responsibility to make sure we have the same success at preserving our way of life the next time. The next time will be different; the odds are high that the next terrorist attack will not involve flying planes with full fuel tanks into buildings. The changed nature of the attack will require a change in the response. But it will not change the likelihood that the nature of your response will have the potential to do more of the terrorists' work for them than will their attack itself. It is useful to contemplate some of the possibilities:

1) Suicide Bombers and Similar Individual Acts

The wave of suicide bombings in Israel during 2001 and 2003 at a time of economic contraction provoked a lot of discussion that this could be the next wave of terror activities in America. There were even a number of suicide-bombing scares at shopping malls. Although frightening events, the actual threat they pose to our way of life is small given a proper response.

The United Kingdom also endured a long series of small-scale terrorist attacks by the Irish Republican Army throughout the 1970s, 1980s, and 1990s. Prime Minister Margaret Thatcher narrowly escaped one of these attacks when the hotel in which she was staying was blown up. Nonetheless, Britain continued to grow economically.

America itself suffers from similar attacks, although they are generally perpetrated by individual nut cases rather than an organized political motive. In 2002, for example, a pair of gunmen terrorized the suburbs of Washington for several weeks with a wave of isolated shootings. And in 2007, a disturbed student killed thirty-two people at Virginia Tech. Although news coverage and discussion of these events is extensive, they are treated appropriately as individual law enforcement events. The only difference in response between this law enforcement treatment and what would be appropriate for a terror-driven wave with an apparent common political motive would be the search for a "mastermind" or command. That is an appropriate assignment for the FBI, which would doubtless be called in early in any event, and for an international intelligence effort should a foreign-inspired motive seem likely.

2) Multiple Incidents Involving Thousands of Deaths

One of the most frightening possibilities in the weeks immediately after 9/11 was that it would happen again. Indeed, one reason that 9/11 itself was so frightening was that it involved four separate plane hijackings, three of which were successful in destroying buildings nearly simultaneously in two different cities. Multiple related incidents are more frightening—provoke more terror—because they establish the fear that death could happen anywhere and at any time in the future. Multiple attacks on London's subways in July 2005 had a similar, albeit shorter-lived, effect. When one can connect multiple dots, it is natural to extrapolate into the future. By contrast, an individual incident strikes the psyche as just that, a one-off event that couldn't possibly affect anyone but those already killed.

The human response to this is an increase in caution far beyond what the mere statistics would suggest. It took real courage to go out of one's house and into work in Manhattan or Washington on Wednesday September 12, 2001. In fact, many people understandably did not show up. What if on Friday, September 14, or on Monday the 17th a car bomb had blown up a tall building in Chicago or Dallas or San Francisco? How many people would continue to show up for work? How many spouses would let wives or husbands commute into downtown metropolitan areas?

There is an international aspect of this that is worth considering. It may not be that all of these attacks must happen in the United States to have their intended terror effect. Suppose, for example, a terrorist attack occurred on a train during the morning commute in Tokyo, say at 8:00 A.M. local time. It would make the 11:00 P.M. news the night before as people were going to bed on the East Coast of America and would dominate the airwaves as people awoke in Europe a few hours later. Suppose that was followed by a similar terrorist incident in Mumbai, India, four hours later, at the height of the morning commute there and as people were just waking up in Europe. Then imagine another, similar attack in Paris. How normal do you think rush hour would be in New York or Washington?

This obviously would involve a wholly different kind of response. Some attempt by you to appeal for calm *that morning* would appear ludicrous. Indeed, events would probably be already out of your hands. Schools would be canceled by local school districts requiring parents to stay home in any event. Some governors might already be declaring holidays for "nonessential" state workers, and individual businesses might be closing voluntarily. It would quickly become a nationwide "snow day" as far as the closings of schools and businesses was concerned.

Our economy and even our way of life can survive such a one-day or even a two- or three-day shutdown. But it cannot survive this as a permanent condition. The appropriate response is draconian but short lived. You will have a mandate in public opinion to change our way of life on a *temporary* basis. This will include police searches, seizures, and interrogations that might not normally be tolerated. But **people will also expect you to sound the "all clear" and a return to normal both rhetorically but also with respect to the behavior of the government in a very short time, ten days or two weeks at most**. That is why you should act immediately not only because the trail of the perpetrators will be clearer but because the sooner you start, the sooner it will all be over. Obviously, catching the perpetrators is a natural event that would signal the all clear.

There are two things that you must do during the period of temporary emergency. **First, there are a number of essential economic services that must continue that you may not think of right away**. One is cash. On 9/11, the Federal Reserve flooded the nation with cash, in part by providing shipments for automated teller machines. With most places of employment shut down, people will immediately seek economic security, and seeking access to their money is an age-old response by people to crisis. If that money is not available, a bank run will start, and that is something that you do not need. While cash needs are immediate, you will need to reopen the banks and the markets in a matter of days, or the basic flow of money will stop in the economy.

The other item that people will flock for in an emergency is food. Grocery stores can be emptied of their contents in less than a day if people are worried—and they will be. Restocking them will require that a significant portion of the transportation and industrial infrastructure be maintained. Note that nearly every family has enough food in their house to last at least several days if not several weeks if they had to. This is not a matter of imminent starvation but one of fear that must be assuaged. You will also need to maintain the energy grid since even if people are in their homes, they will need electricity, natural gas, and even fuel for their cars. You also need to provide a way for people to get home to their families. On any given day, about a million people are away from the metropolitan areas in which they live on business. They will be desperate to get home. In sum, a nationwide curfew, a quarantine, or even imposing limits on the intercity transportation of goods or people are impossibilities for more than the very briefest of periods.

The second item that you must supply is the truth, and only you can do it. The public will tolerate a temporary restriction on their civil and economic liberty if they feel that you are making good use of the time. Some of your subordinates may make mistakes; everyone does. Don't cover them up; acknowledge them and correct them. You also have a responsibility to tell people what happened, who did it, and what you are doing to make sure it doesn't happen again. In addition, treat mistakes as just that, not as criminal acts. One of the surest ways of paralyzing the country is to up the penalty for making the wrong decision. The human response will be to avoid making the wrong decision by making no decisions at all.

3) Weapons of Mass Destruction

This act of terrorism has the greatest risk to our society because it will mean that terrorists have the same capability to deliver destruction as do sovereign states. The key difference between a terrorist state and a sovereign state is that the former does not have territory and population for which it is responsible, so that the single theoretical reason why these weapons are not used—retaliation in kind—no longer applies. America—and all of mankind—will have entered a new era in which the desire for safety again becomes paramount on our hierarchy of needs. **This is by far the most dangerous situation you can face as president since a country that craves the security it no longer possesses is willing to sacrifice both liberty and material well-being.**

The ideal reaction to this situation is similar to the "multiple-incidents" scenario described above. But that may not be possible. First, the lingering damage from the terrorist act will be far greater. This will make a return to normalcy much more difficult. Second, the implied threat of another such incident will make it much more difficult to return to normal without taking unacceptable risks.

In this case, perhaps the best way to approach the issue is to decide what type of America you want to bequeath to your successor as president. It is hoped that that vision is one that maintains essential liberties, both civil and economic. It will be up to you, as leader, to convince the public that there are things as important as some temporary safety. As Ben Franklin artfully said, "Those who would give up essential Liberty, to purchase a little temporary Safety, deserve neither Liberty nor Safety."

THE PROBLEM OF RETALIATION

An attack on American soil by a force that represents no nation-state will call on the greatest leadership skills any president has to offer. Although wars may involve a much more protracted and complicated set of decisions, they provide one of the most important psychological needs a people under attack need: a target to strike back against. Terrorists do not represent nation-states and offer no target.

Obviously, bringing the perpetrators to justice is a necessary step, but it is hardly sufficient. Our judicial process was created to provide a substitute for revenge, to bury it in process, in order to stop a cycle of retaliation that might harm society. In that sense it really was not designed for a barbarous act of terrorism, committed by someone who is so far removed from society that he seeks its destruction. But it is the best we have and is the standard by which we measure our own behavior. As such, though, it leaves a void. Even the death penalty for someone who massacred thousands or tens of thousands of people hardly provides any release of built-up anger at the senseless slaughter. This is especially true when it is carried out when justice has "run its course" perhaps several years after the terrorist attack.

Instead, a president must rally the people on the basis of emotions less primal and more difficult to tap than retaliation. Fortunately, these emotions exist in abundance in the American people. **The model to think about is a natural disaster**. Mother Nature is not a target against which one can retaliate. So the American public channels its energies into help for the victims and palliatives running the gamut from better forecasting to tougher building codes. More important is the model these instances provide for the role the president plays.

PRACTICAL RECOMMENDATIONS FOR THE RECOVERY

PUT YOUR BOOTS IN THE MUD

The public expects your personal involvement. No better demonstration of that exists than the contrast in your predecessor's personal performance after 9/11 and his performance after Hurricane Katrina. In the first instance he was on the ground, commending and rallying those tasked with the grisly job of searching for possible survivors but finding mostly corpses, some of them of their comrades. In the latter case it was a presidential flyover to survey the swath of devastation from the air. The first was thought of as heroic, the second inexcusable.

By his presence on the scene of a disaster the president is making the statement that "this place is safe again." His being there, as someone whom the nation spends a great deal of resources on protecting, is a sign that the trouble is over, a statement, if you will, that lightning will not strike this place twice. At no time was that more true than when he overrode the Secret Service and returned to the White House on the evening of September 11.

But there is more than the return of safety signaled by the president's presence. It is also a call to rally one's courage. It is a statement that "I will not succumb to fear." To the individual citizen watching, the message is telegraphed that if the president has the courage to do that, then I have the courage to go to work tomorrow in a tall sky scraper or rebuild my home or even to put my children on the school bus without fear. Boots in the mud means safety, and it means courage.

MAKE A CALL TO SACRIFICE

After a natural disaster, a president informs the public of a way they can help. It might be by donating blood or sending a contribution to the Red Cross. Obviously, after a terrorist attack, these might be needed. But so might other sacrifices. During World War II, rationing of a wide variety of items was instituted. On a strict cost–benefit basis such rationing showed little economic benefit. But it did convey in the citizenry that they were doing their part. **And a cause in which one is doing his or her part is a cause that one is less likely to desert**.

It has been noted that the Iraq War was America's first in which the soldiers were fighting but the country was not. If one did not watch the news, it would be hard to even know the nation was at war. In Vietnam, with more than fifteen times the number of body bags coming home to a country with one-third fewer people than at present, it was hard not to be confronted with the reality of sacrifice. In the Gulf War of 1990, the public noted a spike in gasoline prices that was tied directly to the war. Today, Gulf Coast hurricanes, domestic refinery accidents, a growing Chinese economy, and the taste for risk by financial speculators dominate gas price fluctuations.

It is certainly true that government can come up with some economically crazy ideas for imposing sacrifice on people. The odd–even system for when you could buy gas rationing and the red and green flags were a source of frustration, inefficiency, and ultimately ridicule during the Carter administration. But a *modest* gasoline tax—ten cents per gallon, for example—that was "dedicated" to filling the strategic petroleum reserve or spent on research for alternative fuels might make more sense. Modesty is paramount, as you must be cautious of the contractionary economic effect during a fragile time.

Of course, it is better if the sacrifice is voluntary. During World War II, volunteer air-raid wardens were set up in towns across the country. Neither Tojo nor Hitler would have been deterred in the slightest from attacking any small town in the middle of nowhere because their planes would be spotted by the trusty local warden. But the time committed by those wardens was a sacrifice that allowed them to feel a part of the war effort. Similarly, the collection of aluminum cookware and other forms of scrap collection did little to advance the war effort, but hundreds of thousands of schoolchildren became involved.

It is also best if the sacrifice does not seem for a frivolous purpose. Today, the public is more educated and the press more cynical than during World War II. But sacrifices related to demands on the health care system to channel resources into the fight against biological warfare agents would certainly seem helpful if that were the nature of the attack. Extensive first-aid instruction and voluntary "medical responders" would meet a need following virtually any kind of terrorist attack. Whatever your choice of program, if they feel the act is genuinely helping, the American people will be willing to sacrifice after a terrorist attack, and such sacrifice will provide a healthy outlet for the anger and frustration that they feel.

STAY INFORMED

One of the easiest things to forget as president during a crisis is that a real leader listens as well as commands. While the president is leading the nation, a variety of other, perhaps lesser leaders are carrying out the more narrowly defined tasks that actually make our country function. For your commands to resonate effectively, they should reflect the realities observed by these other leaders.

For example, business leaders know what is actually happening in the economy and how your policies are working in practice. When listening to them, you must get past the praise they will bestow about being behind you and listen for the subtle undercurrents of what is not working. The same is true with your party's state and local leadership. This includes both holders of public office and party officials. They provide a natural network to hear what people are actually thinking.

The same is true of parts of the news media. Newspaper editors and talk show hosts alike will provide valuable insights into what people are really thinking. Your press office may try to shield you from these people by offering to play the role of intermediary. But having your press office listen is quite different from you listening yourself. By and large, media people will be willing to play by the rules you set in your conversations, and you can easily reinforce that by excluding those who do not.

By being on the scene, asking for sacrifices, and taking time to listen, you will be providing the leadership the country needs at this particularly crucial time.

MAINTAIN CONFIDENCE

One of your most important roles after an attack will be maintaining confidence. This is crucial to keeping the economy growing in the aftermath. Al-Qaeda and other terrorist groups clearly understand that the core strength of the United States is its economic position in the world and would like nothing more than to put us into depression. The World Trade Center was chosen as a target because it symbolized our global economic leadership. Osama bin Laden picked the target not just once, on 9/11, but also in 1993, when al-Qaeda tried to blow it up using truck bombs.

Part of proving that America prevailed over the terrorists is to maintain economic growth. This does not mean you should be

Pollyannaish. Nothing will hurt confidence more than a leader who looks like he is out of touch. You must acknowledge our challenges while clearly laying out the specific actions that you will take to protect our economy.

Your predecessor was fortunate in one respect. Fiscal stimulus was hitting at the time of the attack and helped the economy recover faster than it would have. In fact, consumption spending rebounded so quickly in the fourth quarter of 2001 that we had the largest drawdown of inventories ever. If not for the tax cuts, the recession of the time would undoubtedly have been much deeper and more prolonged and confidence damaged on a more permanent basis.

Shortly after the attack, a bipartisan group was convened in the Office of the Speaker of the House to discuss the possibility of more economic stimulus. It included the congressional leaders of both parties, myself, Alan Greenspan, and Robert Rubin, among others. I represented a minority view in favor of erring on the side of more economic stimulus given that the downside risks were obviously greater than any upside potential. The dominant view was to collect more data for another month to get a better feel for what was happening. This bipartisan process did ultimately produce another tax cut that included a temporary stimulus to investment and some needed economic assistance to the unemployed, but it took six months to accomplish. To this day it seems surprising that even in the post-9/11 atmosphere, it took six months. After all, it had taken the president only four months in office to enact his much bigger tax plan in May 2001.

A SOUND ECONOMY IS A PUBLIC GOOD

Political ideologies vary about the appropriate role for government, but one theme exists across the political spectrum. The government can and must provide for things that individual participants in our economy cannot. These items are called public goods. Security against a terrorist attack or foreign aggression is one such good. Individuals cannot and should not be expected to protect themselves either physically or financially against an attack by a foreign power. Economic confidence is one aspect of this, which is the case for fiscal stimulus if confidence is fading after an attack.

But the failure of the government to provide security against a terrorist attack also puts an obligation on the government to assist in ameliorating the losses suffered from such an attack. For example, the airline industry was grounded by government decree on 9/11. It was a sensible and necessary move given the risks of that day. But the costs of the airline industry continued to run despite the grounding. They still had to make payments on the loans and leases they took out to acquire the airplanes. Most of their employees continued to draw paychecks. Rental expenses at airports continued. Cutting off the revenue that paid for these costs was not a company decision dictated by the market; it was a government decision based on a failure to protect against a terrorist attack. Moreover, getting passengers to decide to fly again with memories of 9/11 fresh was not going to be an easy task.

There are a number of ideological reasons to have just let the airline industry go bankrupt. Some, particularly on the political left, oppose bailing out big business. Some, particularly on the political right, argue that a market system is a profit-and-loss system and that this is a risk inherent in doing business. While the bankruptcy process works as a general rule, the losses suffered by the industry were incurred not because of any fault of their own but because of a failure to provide a basic public good: security. Moreover, letting the airline industry fail would have been a symbolic blow to confidence that could become self-reinforcing. A terrorist attack is no time to let ideology drive policy.

A similar situation existed in the case of terrorism risk insurance for large buildings. This was almost an afterthought on most insurance policies before 9/11 because it was a rare event. After 9/11, the apparent risks to insure such buildings skyrocketed. One could make the ideological case that this heightened risk meant that it was economically efficient to have fewer high-rise office buildings that made inviting targets. But this begs the question: Should Americans have to base their private decisions on the chance that airplanes might fly into the buildings where they work, or should they assume that this is a responsibility for government? You will find it much easier to restore confidence in the economy and in the willingness of the government to provide for basic security if you treat such items as public goods.

RELAX REGULATORY
CONSTRAINTS IF NECESSARY

For all its freedoms, the U.S. economy is still highly regulated. There are hundreds of thousands of rules that we have learned to live with in normal times. But another lesson of 9/11 was the importance of quickly relaxing economic constraints, when it was possible to do so safely, so that problems can be fixed. After September 11, one of the first orders on the economy that the president gave was to get the financial markets back open. The biggest single problem faced by the financial firms in New York was simply getting technologically savvy people into the buildings so they could figure out what was needed to get trading again.

This was not going to be easy given the state of lower Manhattan and the amount of government regulations that potentially stood in the way. For example, select workers needed permission from environmental regulators to be in the disaster area and needed to obtain proper equipment since the air quality standards in lower Manhattan were potentially dangerous. Electric power was needed. While the City of New York had located needed generators, it was unable to get them where they were needed. The National Economic Council (NEC) alerted the Department of Transportation that permits were needed so that wide-load flatbed trucks could carry them, an otherwise prohibited act. The NEC found tugboats to deliver the generators to the island of Manhattan. There were also requirements that all power and communications lines had to be underground. That is hardly a simple task, so the NEC helped secure permission for the affected companies to run their lines down the street on a temporary basis and tape them to the sidewalk. This was an obvious safety hazard on a permanent basis, but applying normal safety precautions in a de facto war zone just doesn't make sense.

Under the law, the White House cannot simply order that regulations be waived. But it can convey a sense of urgency and of priorities to the agencies that do control these regulations. What will happen after a terrorist attack is that the country will devolve temporarily into a command-and-control economy because of the number of things that need to be done that cannot be done in a timely fashion because of the everyday rules under which we operate. Nor can your White House staff function for long as the de facto Kremlin of the country. If that were a system that actually worked, the Berlin Wall would still be standing. An executive order allowing common-sense responses to emergency conditions would certainly be helpful should another terrorist attack occur.

REINFORCE STAFF MORALE

While you are leading the nation, you will also be leading the building. Your White House staff will be watching you for how they should respond. If you are brave, they will be brave. If you are calm, they will be calm. It's important to remember the stress they will be under as well. The White House, after all, attracts a lot of young talent—who else is willing to work the hours?—and most of them will not be used to working under emergency conditions. The constant reminders of the threat, from frequent evacuations to taking Cipro to ward off the effects of possible anthrax exposure, all take their toll.

You will be surprised and no doubt humbled by their loyalty. In the days after the events, one of my staff who was married with children said, "Give me a chem suit and an American flag and I'll never leave my desk." And he wasn't kidding. But most will not be of the same timber that you are—it's what separates the president from staff after all—and letting them know you appreciate their sacrifice and courage is important to your team's morale.

AT THE HELM
OF THE ECONOMY

I F YOU READ the bio on the dust jacket before buying the book, you're probably aware that when it comes to watching the downside of the business cycle from a political perspective, I am probably in contention for the *Guinness Book of World Records*. I have served in three different White Houses. Each time there was a recession. It's enough to give a guy a complex. But I doubt there is any cause and effect. Most important, two of the three presidents I worked for were able, through a combination of sound policy and the passage of time, to produce a sufficient economic revival to get reelected.

When it comes to the overall economy, good policy and the passage of time are inextricably linked. The American economy operates like a supertanker. The momentum is tremendous. It takes a long time to stop, a long time to turn, and, for that matter, a long time to get going again once it does stop. It needs periodic servicing and checks of its structural integrity. It also has limits as to its capacity and its range, and when you approach those limits, it is time to watch out. But because it takes so long to alter either speed or direction, economic policymakers need to have very long run views about the dangers that lie ahead.

If the American economy were to have a room like the bridge of a supertanker, it would doubtless be the meeting room of the Board of Governors of the Federal Reserve. The boardroom sits on the second floor of the Eccles Building, facing Constitution Avenue, almost across the street from the Vietnam Memorial. It has the potential for providing a nice view. But during meetings of the Federal Open Market Committee (FOMC), the heavy curtains are drawn. The reason is security. Carefully calibrated devices can pick up the vibrations from windows, which, with computer enhancement, can be turned into transcripts of the meetings being held. Drawing the floor-to-ceiling curtains makes that impossible. It also lends an air of both solemnity and mystery to the proceedings inside.

On September 24, 1996, the FOMC was in session, and I was in one of my meddlesome moods. As a governor of the Federal Reserve System, I had a permanent voting membership on the FOMC. The economy was doing well, and inflation seemed well contained. The stock market was rising rapidly. As governors, we had just had a briefing from leading Wall Street analysts predicting that corporate profit growth going forward would average 11.5 percent per year for the next five years, just like it had for the last five. This, the analysts said, would fully justify a continued rise in the stock market. And indeed it would.

Trouble was, 11.5 percent profit growth for the next five years would take the corporate profit share of gross domestic product (GDP) so high that something would have to give. It would be like running a supertanker's engine at high revolutions per minute for hours on end. In the end, what would have to give economically was wages, after adjusting for inflation, and given that the labor market was tightening, this seemed unlikely. So I said that the prediction of continued profit growth was nonsense. Actually, these are very restrained meetings, and the tone is decidedly understated. The actual quote was, "Readers of this transcript in five years can check this fearless prediction: profits will fall short of this expectation."[1]

My concern wasn't really about profits; it was about the stock market. If profits were not going to rise (in fact, profit margins fell nearly in half over the next five years), the rise in the stock market was not justified. It was in the early stages of forming a bubble. A financial bubble is one in which the price of assets rise without regard to the fundamental value of the asset but merely on the expectation that someone will come along and pay an even higher price. This is sometimes called "the Greater Fool Theory." Since the underlying value of a stock is its long-run ability to pay dividends to its owner and since a company can't pay dividends unless it is profitable, the prospect for profits over the next five years was crucial for determining whether the stock market's rise was justified or was merely a bubble.

The problem with bubbles historically is that they tend to create both economic and social distortions. At its extremes, individuals tend to abandon their usual economic pursuits to devote their energies to gambling in the financial markets. The day-trader phenomenon was an example of this. Corporations find that their run-of-the-mill pursuits of making goods and marketing them yield lower returns than bubble-crazed investors might want. Corporate energies are poured into the accounting and finance departments, which often begin to devote their energies to finding ways of wringing reported profits from the rapidly changing prices of financial assets, often to the detriment of honest evaluation of their core businesses.

When the bubble bursts, some individuals who had a good sense of timing become fantastically wealthy. Others lose their life savings. The apparent randomness of the result undermines faith in hard work, creativity, and entrepreneurship as the cornerstones of success. The political reaction is often to pass laws to make sure "it never happens again," laws that are frequently guilty of overreach. The net effect of such laws is not to prevent future bubbles but to enrich those with the legal or lobbying skills to find ways around them.

So if I sound like a bit of a moralist about the evils of financial bubbles, I probably am. My only defense is that they have a long history of ending badly. So in my best moralistically meddlesome tone, I went on with my lecture at the FOMC meeting. "The long term costs of a bubble to the economy and society are potentially great.... As in the United States in the late 1920s and in Japan in the late 1980s, the case for a central bank to ultimately burst that bubble becomes overwhelming. I think it far better that we do so while the bubble still represents surface froth and before the bubble carries the economy to stratospheric heights."[2]

I was calling for the Fed to raise rates or at least think about it. Chairman Alan Greenspan said, "I recognize that there is a stock market bubble problem at this point, and I agree with Governor Lindsey that this is a problem that we should keep an eye on. We have very great difficulty in monetary policy when we confront stock market bubbles. That is because, to the extent that we are successful in keeping product price inflation down, history tells us that price-earnings ratios under those conditions go through the roof."[3]

I raise this story not merely to moralize about the evils of bubbles but to illustrate the interaction of time and policy and to show how long the lead times can be. Three and a half years before the bubble actually burst—indeed, while it was still in its early stages of formation—policymakers were already aware of the potential threat that lay ahead. It was a bit like having a conversation on the bridge of a supertanker saying, "We're about to cross the sixtieth parallel; we should be prepared to watch for icebergs." There is no substitute for being prepared for risks early.

A year and a half later, in April 1998, Chairman Greenspan and I sat in his office discussing the bubble. I had left the Board of Governors in early 1997 and was writing a book about economic decision making called *Economic Puppetmasters*.[4] The British magazine *The Economist* had as its cover story "America's Bubble Economy."

Knowledge of the problem ahead had moved from the rarified atmosphere of the Federal Reserve boardroom to the international high-brow media. It is always easier seeing a bubble from the outside; it is rarely obvious when you are stuck inside. Meanwhile, the general public was actively buying stock in any company with a "dot-com" in its name. And profits in the nonfinancial corporate sector were beginning a protracted fall, not rising at double-digit rates, as the Wall Street experts had predicted.

I asked Greenspan about the bubble and its likely aftermath. His answer was a lesson in the timing of economic policy that was crucial: "1929 did not cause 1933. It depends on what you do in 1930 and 1931." It was also a point that, in hindsight, led me to agree with Greenspan about the appropriate course of monetary policy. Bubbles do provide a positive function: they move capital into high-risk ventures, including new technologies, which may produce high long-run returns.

A bubble in the 1920s had facilitated the spread of the automobile and the development of radio. It had ended very badly, but only because policymakers were unprepared and ended up doing the wrong thing. If policymakers were prepared, it might, in the end, be smarter to allow the bubble to develop, bring new technologies to market, and then use appropriate fiscal and monetary policies to clean up the mess later.

What had actually happened in 1930 and 1931 was that Congress had seen the budget deficit worsen as the stock market and the economy weakened. They chose to raise taxes dramatically. All tax rates were increased by at least 70 percent more than their previous level. They also sharply raised tariffs on imports. Moreover, the Federal Reserve Board did not ease the stance of monetary policy but actually let the money supply fall as economic conditions deteriorated. The lesson was clear: do the opposite of what happened in the early 1930s should the equity bubble break. If one was going to clean up the mess rather than make it worse, the right thing to do was cut taxes, avoid protectionism, and ease monetary conditions.

During that year I was also flying to Austin to do economic briefings for the then governor of Texas, George W. Bush. When we got to the prospects of a stock market bubble, he reminded me that he had been in the oil industry in Texas in the mid-1980s. He knew all about bubbles bursting and their terrible aftermath. He remembered what happened in Midland, Texas: families losing their jobs, their life savings, and sometimes their homes. He also knew that should he become president, he didn't want that to happen under his watch.

So, on December 1, 1999, in Des Moines, Iowa, he gave one of the most remarkably timed speeches that I can remember. It was almost the very peak of the bubble. Many economists were talking about the repeal of the business cycle. But Bush said, "Yet I also believe in tax cuts for another practical reason: because they provide insurance against economic recession. Sometimes economists are wrong. I can remember recoveries that were supposed to end but didn't. And recessions that weren't supposed to happen but did. I hope for continued growth—but it is not guaranteed."

The Dow Jones Industrial Average peaked one month later on January 14, 2000. The NASDAQ peaked three months later on March 10 at a level of 5,130. Three months after that, the economy started its first quarterly decline in nine and a half years. By the time Bush took office, the NASDAQ had fallen 50 percent from its peak.

But Bush had his "insurance policy" already drafted and ready for congressional consideration, and it was signed into law in early June. The first rebate checks from the tax cut were received by Americans in late July and August, just before the September 11 terrorist attacks. Despite the events of that day and the uncertainty it created, Americans did what economic theory predicted they would: spend the money they had just gotten in the mail. Consumption spending grew 7 percent in the fourth quarter of 2001, the biggest consumer-led surge since 1986.

The economy is slow to turn. Moreover, James Madison designed our Constitution to make government policy slow to turn as well. So, when it comes to economic policy, there is no substitute for being prepared and knowing what you're going to have to accomplish before you get there.

What follows is what I told the president-elect he had better decide very quickly if he is going to successfully steer the supertanker of the American economy through the next four years.

MEMORANDUM FOR THE PRESIDENT

FROM: LAWRENCE B. LINDSEY
SUBJECT: THREE ECONOMIC DECISIONS YOU NEED TO MAKE SOON
January 20, 2009

Most of the economic challenges facing America are long term in nature: our competitive position in the world and the challenges facing middle-class families are but two examples. You discussed them endlessly on the campaign trail and will be proposing policies to address them throughout your term. Ultimately, though, **there is one economic challenge for which you absolutely will be held accountable: maintaining economic growth during your watch**.

Consider the odds. Each of the last seven presidents had at least one-quarter of economic decline during his presidency. Three of them, Nixon, Reagan, and the current President Bush, had them early enough in their presidencies that they could take policy measures to reverse them in time for their reelection. One, Clinton, had an economic decline late in his very last year that spilled over into his successor's term. The other three, Ford, Carter, and the first President Bush, were defeated in large part because of economic circumstances.

Moreover, by this metric, the current economic expansion is getting old. The last quarter in which this economy contracted was in 2001! That was eight years ago. Since the end of World War II, the average period without a negative quarter was only two years. The longest such period was nine and a half years, during the 1990s, when we had just cleaned up the banking system, had a sustained period of favorable monetary policy, and had a major period of technological innovation.

You can leave things to chance, or you can attempt to control your fate by making decisions early in three key areas. In each case, a decision will be forced on you by events. And each of these three have impacted the performance of the economy during the terms of one or more of your predecessors:

- Leadership at the Federal Reserve
- Tax policy
- Dollar policy

THE CURRENT BUSINESS CYCLE

An earlier memo considered the role played by image consultants in your administration. They have their role, but in the end, **substance trumps spin**. Your spinners are probably out in force right now saying that now that you have had a chance to really "look at the books," things are much worse than what you thought. This is a time-honored tradition in both business and politics whenever there is a turnover at the top: blame your predecessor. It sets up a low base of expectations and makes it easier for you to exceed them.

Ironically, your predecessor had the opposite experience in 2001. Things really were worse than anyone thought. On January 3, before he became president, at a closed-door meeting in Austin with America's business leaders, the president-elect was told universally by those in attendance that the economy was falling off a cliff. The Federal Reserve reached the same conclusion, making what was the first of thirteen interest rate cuts on the same day. Later, the government came out and revised its statistics showing that rather than having the robust growth they had reported, the economy actually contracted in the quarter before Election Day. **Whatever your spin, it will not change the fundamentals**.

On an actuarial basis, this expansion is getting old. It is true that economic expansions do not die of old age. But people don't either. Over time, the systems that sustain growth just become less and less efficient. Finally, something fails. Below is a chart of two key indicators of the efficiency with which the economy is expanding: productivity and unit labor costs.

	2002	2003	2004	2005	2006
Productivity growth	4.1	3.7	2.7	1.9	1.0
Growth in hours worked	-2.6	-0.6	1.4	1.6	2.2
Unit labor costs	-0.5	0.3	0.9	2.0	2.9

Productivity measures the growth in the average output per hour of workers in the nonfarm business sector, the real engine of economic growth. Early in an expansion, businesses are "lean and mean." They have just survived the last recession, a period in which their less efficient competitors went out of business. Not only have the least efficient parts of the economy disappeared, but the survivors are acting like they have just had a near-death experience. They are ruthlessly shedding any unnecessary cost they can and getting as much output as possible out of what is left.

Then, as the economic expansion matures, both the psychology of "lean and mean" and the possibilities of acting that way begin to disappear. No one really likes to make tough decisions like firing someone or closing down a factory. Despite the "tough-guy" image of a lot of businessmen, only the real oddball chooses to inflict economic pain needlessly. More important, as output expands, firms need to hire workers. The new workers are likely to be less efficient than the current workforce. Not only do they have to be trained (which is a costly process), but the workers whom the firm retained during the lean times are the best there are. Almost by definition, the new workers hired are going to be less good than the ones working for the firm at the start of the expansion.

The same economic forces are at work in the "unit labor cost" measure. This measures the expenses like wages and benefits for each unit of production. Obviously, if each new worker is producing less efficiently than the workers who are already there (declining productivity) and you are paying the new ones as much as the old ones, then costs per unit are going to rise. But another factor augments this trend: rising wages. As the expansion gets older and more workers are employed, it gets tougher to find new workers. So wages rise. This is simple supply and demand. **Late in an economic expansion, unit labor costs begin to rise sharply because not only are new workers less efficient but the wages for all workers are forced up as well.**

There is absolutely nothing wrong with rising incomes. It is a sign of prosperity. But higher unit labor costs can be financed in only one of two ways: higher prices or lower profits. Usually the process starts with falling profits. For example, late in the expansion in the 1990s, the acceleration in real wages that started late in 1997 was financed by a halving of profit margins over the next four years. The trouble is that profits are the lifeblood of economic expansions, as they finance new economic activity, and when they get too low, the expansion stops, as it did in late 2000. Nor do firms take the process of declining profits quietly. They try to raise prices. Usually they can get away with it since most of their competitors face the same problem. (In the late 1990s the sharp rise in imports from China and other low-wage countries cut this possibility off.) But **the usual consequence of higher unit labor costs is inflation**.

DECISION #1: LEADERSHIP AT THE FEDERAL RESERVE

This is where the Federal Reserve comes into the picture. The action forcing event for your administration will be that **Federal Reserve Chairman Ben Bernanke's chairmanship is up just over one year from today: January 31, 2010.** You will have essentially two options:

1. Reappoint Bernanke
2. Appoint someone with closer ties to you, your party, or your administration

The Federal Reserve has a variety of legal mandates. One is to maintain the integrity of the banking system. Another is economic stabilization. This means that the Fed has a responsibility to stop inflation from getting going when the economy is too hot and to stop unemployment from getting too high when the economy is slowing. When the Fed talks about "high levels of resource utilization" in their policy statements, as they frequently did in 2006 and 2007, they are really saying they are worried about tight labor markets forcing up unit labor costs. It is a warning signal. More important, the Fed has only blunt instruments, and attempted slowdowns have a history of sometimes becoming contractions.

Politically, both you and the Fed will share the blame for a slowing economy, should it occur. Many of your advisers will urge you to shift as much of the blame on to the Fed as possible. After all, you and the members of your party in Congress are up for election; the Federal Reserve is not. There is a (probably true) story from the 1960s about a lunch between Federal Reserve Chairman William McChesney Martin and House Banking Committee Chairman Wright Patman. Patman used to give stem-winding speeches about how awful the Fed was, but he never let any legislation harmful to the Fed out of his committee. Martin asked him why. Patman replied, "If we didn't have you to blame, what would we do?"

Some of your advisers will doubtless argue that, implicitly, by reappointing him, you will be endorsing his performance. You will therefore not have Patman's ability of simply blaming the Fed since it will be more difficult for you to separate yourself from Bernanke. Moreover, some of your closest economic advisers themselves may want the position. It is the highest-ranking job in economic policy-making in the country and in the world.

RECOMMENDATION: Reappoint Bernanke. Changing Fed chairmen involves a cost. **Markets will (correctly) think that the new person is more beholden to you than was Bernanke and will assume that he or she is going to be less vigilant about fighting inflation.** The result will be that the markets will take intermediate- and longer-term interest rates up even more than what they would have if Bernanke had stayed. The new person, faced with a market vote of "no confidence" and rising inflation expectations, will end up raising rates *at least as much* as Bernanke would have. **So you end up with higher** rates and more economic pain—which will translate into more political pain—by getting someone new. There is nothing you can do about the timing of the business cycle at this point, but you can certainly avoid making things worse by making the Federal Reserve appear political.

DECISION #2: THE EXPIRATION OF THE BUSH TAX CUTS

Back in 2001, President Bush got Congress to pass a set of tax cuts to combat the economic slowdown that had developed just before he came to office. The only way to get the tax cuts through the Senate was to pass them as part of budget reconciliation, but that meant that they could not be permanent and had to expire at the end of ten years: right in the middle of your term at the end of 2010. **No matter what you may have said about the Bush tax cuts during your political career, their expiration poses both a problem and an opportunity for you.**

The problem is that unless they are extended—or something quite like them is passed in their place—the economy will face a major fiscal shock. Work by Professors Paul and Christina Romer of Stanford University[5] suggests that the expiration of the Bush tax cuts will, by itself, cut almost four and a half percentage points from GDP. So letting the tax cuts lapse risks losing the equivalent of a full year and a half of growth and sending unemployment up about two and a quarter percentage points, or three and a half million workers. Given the age of the expansion, this could mean a self-induced recession.

The opportunity is that you can pass something else to take its place that is better calibrated to the economic challenges you face in your term. There is the added benefit that it will have your name on it. Again—I don't mean to be too cynical—simply extending a program that has your predecessor's name on it doesn't exactly make your mark in history. More important to the country, the economic circumstances today are different from what they were in 2001. At a minimum, your proposal should be tailored to today's challenges. Even better, you have a fabulous opportunity to fundamentally restructure the tax system in a way that will permanently increase economic growth. This opportunity is so important that I have relegated it to a separate memo.

You have three main options:

1. You can let the tax cuts expire and use the resulting revenue for new or expanded spending programs or for deficit reduction.
2. You can simply extend the tax cuts, making some minor alterations.
3. You can use the expiration of the tax cuts as well as the need for changing the alternative minimum tax as an opportunity to substantially reform the entire tax system.

RECOMMENDATION: Use the money for tax reform. See memo with suggestions later in this briefing book should you choose this route.

RECOMMENDATION: Whatever you do, start the process now and make your intentions clear. Ideally, your policy proposals should be delivered in a nationally televised speech on or before April 15 of this year.

The Bush tax cuts were calibrated to minimize the adverse impact on the economy of the collapse of the stock market bubble of the late 1990s. It had three parts. First, it had a significant reduction in taxes and increases in real take-home pay for middle-income families with children. A four-person family earning the median income got a $1,600 tax cut, an increase in their real income equivalent to the raises they got during two full years of the late 1990s. This kept their incomes up and provided a cushion for their spending during what would inevitably be lean times for their employers. Second, it cut rates on entrepreneurial income to sustain the cash flow of the unincorporated business sector. Third, it raised after-tax returns in the stock market by cutting capital gains and dividend taxation. We estimated that this added about 800 points to the Dow. Aside from being good tax policy, this increase in the stock market sustained corporate pension plans and allowed corporations to invest free cash flow in plant and equipment rather than simply shoring up their pension plans as the collapsing bubble dragged them down. **Simply letting the tax cuts lapse throws these three developments into reverse**. So not only will you have the direct fiscal impact of the resulting hike in taxes, but you will add stress directly to key parts of the economy as well. Even a complete overhaul of the tax system must be careful not to destroy the incentive effects that are now in place as a result of the tax cut.

Using the funds for new spending programs appears to offer a way to minimize the pure fiscal hit of raising taxes. But spending programs take time to get up and running well, and funding them with the expiration of the tax cuts will still demand the redeployment of vast resources from their current private sector use to the new programs. There will be substantial friction involved for the economy. You may still have an ideological predisposition to do this or political commitments to fulfill, but be prepared.

Whatever you do, quick action by you offers a number of advantages. First, **your proposal will shape the debate**. It is an institutional fact of life in the American Constitution that the executive will produce a more coherent proposal—and one more geared to the national interest—than will Congress. Congress is designed to represent a variety of interests, so if you do not propose something, the various and shifting special interests within the legislative process will take charge. **Congress will obviously make changes in whatever you propose, but your proposal will be the high-water mark in economically coherent and sensible legislating**. Moreover, even if you make your proposals very soon, it will take Congress months to enact any legislation. As 2010 is an election year, passing anything will be more difficult then. So, unless you fashion a proposal by early spring, the chances of getting coherent legislation through before the expiration of the tax cuts at the end of 2010 will be greatly reduced.

Second, **individuals, companies, and markets need to know what is coming in order to have time to adjust**. Investment decisions by firms, portfolio decisions by individuals, and plans to start businesses all lie in the balance. Adjustments take time. An extreme example is the "death tax," which will go from a rate of zero to a top rate of 55 percent at the stroke of midnight on December 31, 2010. There is a joke making the rounds that you certainly don't want to celebrate New Year's Eve at your children's house that year. While the more macabre implications may not materialize, there is real injustice and inequity in having some people lose half their life's savings simply because they lived another twenty-four hours. In a vibrant economy, people need to have time to make plans, including plans about their estates. Moreover, while it has dramatic effects on some individuals, changes in the death tax are not even the most economically damaging of the tax changes that will occur. **More time means lower adjustment costs**.

DECISION #3: DOLLAR POLICY

The exchange value of the dollar in international markets is one of the most important determinants of the near-term competitiveness of our industries and of the overall performance of our capital markets. Except in a few cases where foreign countries actively manage the value of their currencies by buying and selling, markets set the exchange value of the dollar. The exchange rate is the key price in our economy, and flexibility in this price helps stabilize the economy. **But markets are very sensitive to signals from policymakers in how they price currencies**.

The most famous example of this was in the early Clinton administration when Treasury Secretary Lloyd Bentsen made comments that markets interpreted as desiring a "weak dollar." The dollar plummeted. In the end, that provided a stimulus to the U.S. economy that helped it in 1994, but it also laid the groundwork for a number of financial crises later in the decade: Mexico in 1994 and Asia in 1997. This ultimately led to the adoption of a "strong dollar" mantra by Bentsen's successor, Robert Rubin.

From a strictly economic perspective, there is no right and wrong value of the dollar. It depends crucially on your other economic policies. For example, a weak dollar policy will spur American exports but will probably cause interest rates to rise, hurting domestic interest-sensitive industries like housing. By and large, given the size of the current account deficit and the large inflow of foreign money into the United States, the evidence suggests that the dollar is too high. The dollar is likely to fall and at some point fall sharply. So **you are likely to experience some wide fluctuations in the currency's value during your administration**. If there is no guidance on the dollar, these wide swings will create a perception that your administration is "not in charge," which, if there are other problems, may complicate your political situation.

But there is another important consideration. The dollar is the world's reserve currency, as two-thirds of all international reserves are held in dollars. America derives enormous benefits from this fact in our ability to easily finance our fiscal needs in world markets. Moreover, the debt that your government will issue is priced in dollars and is increasingly sold to foreigners. A decision by you to intentionally devalue the currency will be seen by these foreign holders effectively as a partial default. At the beginning of our nation, Alexander Hamilton made a momentous choice to pay off all the war debt of the states rather than let them default. He called the debt a blessing, seeing an opportunity to establish the credibility of a young nation. You should follow Hamilton's guide and protect the integrity of U.S. debt.

It is far easier to lower the value of the currency by saying adverse comments than to raise it. You and your administration have a moral responsibility to international investors who hold dollar assets and to future generations of Americans not to destroy confidence in the dollar. Markets may take the exchange value of the dollar higher or lower, but they should do so on the basis of their assessments of the fundamentals, not on the basis of the political risk coming from the mouths of government officials.

RECOMMENDATION: Set a dollar policy and make sure everyone sticks to it but don't deliberately talk the value of the dollar down.

In the Bush administration, the policy went something like this. (1) We believed in a strong dollar. (2) We believed that markets should set the value of the dollar and opposed intervention to manipulate the markets. (3) A strong dollar requires open and free movements of goods and capital, and we pursued policies to promote them. (4) A strong dollar is one that maintains its purchasing power, and therefore we supported the anti-inflationary policies of the Federal Reserve.

Whatever the actual talking points you and your advisers develop, everyone has to stick to them and say the same thing, or markets will become confused. The U.S. economy will pay a price, and so will your political fortunes.

CHAPTER

SEVEN

❦

A WORLD OF
POROUS BORDERS

A MAJORITY OF the Lindsey family are immigrants, as all three of our children were born overseas. Or, as we jokingly say, our children didn't arrive by a stork but by 747. Troy, our oldest, comes from Bulgaria. Emily comes from Romania, and Tommy, our youngest, comes from Macedonia. Their stories are straight out of the Neil Diamond hit song "They're Coming to America." This background naturally inclines me to be a supporter of immigration; it also gives me some firsthand knowledge of what life is like in the places people are coming from and in the process of becoming an American. Let me share with you some of the insights this experience has brought me.

Silistra lies in the northeastern corner of Bulgaria in the fertile Danube valley. Civilization there pre-dates the Roman conquest of the area in the century before the birth of Christ. We arrived there to get our oldest son, Troy, on his second birthday in late October. Outside, the winter's food supply for the orphanage sat in large piles: root vegetables with which to make soup. I assume that this was augmented with bread. We had brought clothes for Troy that one would normally buy for a two-year-old, but all were pathetically large. He weighed just twenty-two pounds (which didn't even register at the bottom end of the charts at the pediatrician's when we got back home). But he had to change into what we brought since all the clothes he had on were removed to be worn by another child. He was quite stoic about all this until it came to giving up his prize possession—his first pair of shoes—which he had just gotten the week before.

But it was the temperature of the place that got to me—the same low fifties on the inside as on the outside. The director was feverishly calling Sofia, the capital, to try to get some oil for the furnace. We all signed the papers giving us custody of Troy, and then I handed him a check saying from my very faint memories of high school Russian (a close cousin to Bulgarian), "Just buy oil." It was hard enough to leave the other children behind, even worse in a place without heat.

That day, Troy had his first trip outside the orphanage since he was eleven days old. He had never even traveled by car. We had brought juice boxes for him, but he had never used a straw before and, despite being thirsty, didn't know how to drink the contents. When he first saw a television, he watched the actor walk "offstage" and proceeded to go all around the television set looking for where he had gone. It still is hard for me to believe that this happened in Europe in the 1990s. By the way, Troy is now a 190-pound sixteen-year-old who plays football in high school and like many Bulgarians (who excel in these things in international competitions) can deadlift nearly twice his body weight.

Emily hails from a little village about ten miles outside of Bucharest. Bulgaria was poor, but the people cared. Romania was a land of total indifference. Our longtime family friend who was working there pointed out to me the large number of amputees in the general population, a point you could see simply by riding through the streets. "No insulin" was her simple explanation. The recently departed leaders—the Ceaucescus—had also put the country on a plan called "Romania on 900 calories a day." With stringent food rationing, they could actually export some of their own crops to earn the foreign exchange reserves needed to maintain their international position. While I do not normally think of myself as cruel and having seen their legacy, my personal view is that the departure of the Ceaucescus from this world (they were machine-gunned after a show trial) was quite fitting.

Emily had spent the first year of her life in a crib with three other orphans. She could barely sit up and certainly could not stand on her first birthday. At that time, roughly one-quarter of all children born in Romania were left in the hospital, as their parents did not think they had any way of taking care of them. The first time she saw me, she grabbed my sweater and would not let go, sensing perhaps that I was her ticket out of there. The toys and simple medicines that I had brought to the orphanage as gifts for the children simply disappeared overnight. The staff needed them for their own families.

The staff had also warned me to be sure to give Emily whatever she wanted. She had perfected the technique of holding her own breath until she passed out. Even the underpaid and indifferent staff there responded to this, so she doubtless got better attention than the others. This technique had probably made a big difference to her long-term health. Her older brother got her to quit the holding of her breath a couple of years later by telling her that he would just laugh at her if she did it again. But like many fourteen-year-old daughters, she still manages to get just about anything she wants from her father.

Tommy, our youngest, was born in Gostivar, Macedonia, in December 1999. There was a "low-grade" civil war going on in Macedonia at the time between the dominant Slavs and the minority Albanians in what was really a spillover from the much more bloody conflict going on in Kosovo, just across the border. In fact,

Tommy's biological mother had crossed the border into Macedonia on foot to give birth to him there, making him a Macedonian, and then walked back to Kosovo by herself five days later. It was a good thing since Kosovo was being run by the United Nations, which has a policy against foreign adoptions. In fact, the UNICEF bureaucrat in charge of an orphanage there had told our friend, "No rich American is going to adopt any of these children as long as I am in charge." It's a great world, isn't it?

But the civil war in Macedonia was intensifying. When we went to get him in the spring of 2000, a Slavic employee of the Macedonian social services agency simply removed a key document from his file out of spite, making it impossible for us to bring Tommy home. As a result, we had to leave him behind in the orphanage for seven months and go back in December on his first birthday. Thank goodness the delay wasn't longer. Three months after we left, there was a massacre in the lobby of the Holiday Inn in Skopje (Macedonia's capital) where we had stayed. Gostivar itself was the scene of some fierce fighting between the Albanian rebels and the government's Slavic troops.

So our children have escaped from poverty, brutal dictatorships, and civil war. What is astonishing to remember as we sit in comfort here in America is that this kind of background is typical of the immigrants who have come here. Beneath the Statue of Liberty it says, "Give me your tired, your poor, your huddled masses yearning to breathe free." Lady Liberty did not typically hold her torch to those who lived in comfort abroad. Nearly all our ancestors were fleeing poverty, violence, and repression when they came here, be it today or in the past.

Therefore, even as we debate the frustrating problem of illegal immigration, it is important to remember that the people who broke our laws to come here did so not out of malice but out of desperation. When you see where people come from, it is easier to sympathize. This doesn't necessarily make them right, however.

The other side of our experience with immigration is that we've also been through all the paperwork, the waiting on seemingly endless lines, and the confrontations with officious bureaucrats at the Immigration and Naturalization Service (INS; since renamed the Citizenship and Immigration Services). In fact, unlike other immigrants, we haven't just been through the process once; we've done it three separate times.

This gives us a fairly broad set of perspectives on the whole immigration question. It also makes me a skeptic of nearly every immigration "reform" idea that is now being debated. I've gotten on line well before 7:00 in the morning at the Arlington, Virginia, INS office even though the doors didn't open until 8:30 because I learned that if you actually get there when the doors supposedly open, you will have absolutely no chance of getting waited on that day. I've been on hold for four hours at the INS automatic telephone answering service.

So when politicians talk about a "comprehensive plan" to deal with the 11 million illegal immigrants here in this country, I have to chuckle. The INS could barely handle the naturalization of 604,000 people in 2005. At this rate, if you put those 11 million at the back of the *current line* of people here legally waiting to be naturalized or in the legal line to get a green card overseas to come and work here, we wouldn't even get to them until the early 2020s, and the queue would finally be emptied roughly in 2040.

As you may have gleaned from reading some of the memos in this book, I have scant patience for politicians who do not think through issues before enunciating positions. Immigration reform is one of those problems that politicians seem to be less than perfectly knowledgeable about. So I do have some choice words for the next president on this matter, as you shall see in the next memo on globalization.

And while immigration is the most emotive part of globalization, the international flow of ideas and money matter too. They are part of an unyielding trend that the next president will have to manage. Globalization is affecting all of us to a surprising degree. I can't say I ever expected to live in a house of immigrants or that I would travel a quarter of a million miles on an airplane in a single year. Nor could I have predicted that this exposure would make me more pro-America. It has. The more one sees of the rest of the world, the more one appreciates what we have. But life is full of surprises, and the presidency is life at its fullest.

MEMORANDUM FOR THE PRESIDENT

FROM: LAWRENCE B. LINDSEY
SUBJECT: GLOBALIZATION AND THE NATIONAL INTEREST
January 20, 2009

Globalization touches a raw nerve everywhere on this planet. The free movement of ideas, goods, labor, and capital around the world is "subversive." No economic or social trend has the ability to produce such radical change or be more disruptive of the existing order. Established companies who dominate their home markets must now compete for the goodwill of consumers who can choose goods from elsewhere that may be cheaper or of higher quality. Foreign ideologies undermine existing orthodoxies. Both workers and capitalists face threats to comfortable niches they may enjoy.

On balance, **a trend toward globalization is one of the biggest allies America has for advancing its foreign policy, its economy, and its way of life**. There is a reason why foreign tyrannies censor the information available to their citizens and why even democratic countries put content restrictions on filmmaking, music, and other cultural exports of America and why McDonald's and Starbucks are targets for protestors around the world. The same dynamic has made America the preferred destination for the world's most talented people in science, technology, business, and finance. Globalization is the vehicle of economic and political liberty around the planet, and America holds the torch of liberty highest.

But the subversive quality of liberty cuts both ways. American manufacturers find their dominance of our markets undermined. American workers face intense competition from foreign workers who also demand the right to sell the fruits of their labor here. Moreover, tens of millions of people seek to move to our shores to enjoy the benefits of the American way of life and in the process bring with them habits and cultural mores that many Americans resent.

THE PENDULUM OF TOLERANCE

There are few topics in which your ability as president to set the tone of the discussion is more important to both our long-term economic and foreign policy success and to our domestic tranquility. History is of scant comfort. **Both American public opinion and global conditions seem to swing like a pendulum between openness to all things foreign and more inward-looking policies**. The Constitution itself has a nativist clause regarding the office you hold—that the president must be a natural-born citizen of the United States, meaning that he or she can't be an immigrant. Theories abound on this, but one plausible reason was that it was designed to keep Alexander Hamilton, an immigrant from the British West Indies, from holding the office.

Hamilton may have been an immigrant, but he was less than generous to imported goods. Part of his economic vision was the development of domestic industry through tariff protection against imports. His view was popular in most of the North but not in the export-oriented South. Even so, one of the first secession movements in the new Republic was not from the South but from New England, and the issue was international trade. The Jeffersonian-dominated Congress in 1806–1808 passed a series of laws to limit transatlantic trade for foreign policy reasons. The Rhode Island shipbuilding and Massachusetts seafaring industries were devastated, and Vermont, whose main source of economic life was trade northward with British Canada, simply ignored the acts.

Immigration altered the political landscape. The presidential election of 1828 ended the dominance of the old aristocracy of Virginia planters and the Adams family of Massachusetts by installing the Scots-Irish Andrew Jackson in office. During his tenure, there were also widespread riots in large cities, like New York between the "Orange" Scots Irish, who had arrived in the eighteenth century, and the "Green" Catholic Irish, who had just arrived. As discussed in a later memo in this briefing book, nativist concern about the Irish also sparked the public school movement in an effort to control the education of the new—and different—Irish immigrants.

The American canals of this period and the railroads that followed were built with a combination of immigrant labor (Irish and German in the East, Chinese in the West) and British and French capital. Many of the Irish and German railroad workers were paid in land along the railroad, both as a way of saving money and as a source of future customers after the railroad was built. The Chinese fared less well, and ultimately immigration from China was banned by the Chinese Exclusion Act of 1882.

The importation of capital was sponsored by a number of names still familiar today. In Philadelphia, Nicholas Biddle tried to run the Bank of the United States as a private institution after Jackson blocked its recommissioning. The State Street Company in Boston, what is today JPMorgan Chase, was first founded by Aaron Burr in 1799 as the Bank of the Manhattan Company.

The late 1860s showed a particular challenge with "cheap foreign competition" in a major industry: cotton. The Union blockade of the South during the Civil War had cut Britain off from its major supplier of raw cotton. The textile industry of the British Midlands was in trouble. At first, they turned to Egypt as a source of raw cotton but later expanded to Indian cotton—the likely location of the first domestication of cotton 6,000 years ago—but using imported seeds. By the late 1860s and early 1870s, Indian cotton had taken much of the British market, helped in part by British imperial policies. This provided an early example of what we now think of as "unfair trade practices."

Although the United States prospered from imported labor and capital, the dominant view of the late nineteenth century was hostile to importation of foreign goods, a view that provoked sharp partisan divides based largely on the regional divisions that the two parties represented. The Republican Party was dominant in the industrialized North and favored the tariffs, while the Democratic Party of the South and West tended to oppose them. The Morrill tariff of 1861 was considered by some a "payback" to Pennsylvania for supporting Lincoln's election. Republican dominance in the late nineteenth century led to generally high tariffs, although they fell under Democrat Grover Cleveland, only to be raised again under Republican William McKinley. Tariffs were lowered again under Wilson—from roughly 40 percent on average to about 25 percent—when the personal income tax was introduced as a means of covering the revenue losses from the tariff reduction.

But free trade suffered its biggest blow at the onset of the Great Depression with the passage of the Smoot Hawley tariff in 1930. Declining tax revenues and increased import penetration caused Congress to raise the average tariff rate to over 60 percent on thousands of products along with an increase in the top personal income tax rate to 63 percent. The result was a 67 percent drop in world commerce from 1929 to 1933 as other countries retaliated.[1] Partly as a result of this, the pendulum has been swinging in the free trade and low-tariff direction since the end of World War II. Today, the average tariff rate on imports is only 2 percent.

The pendulum also began to swing against immigration in the late nineteenth century, in large part because of the sheer volume of immigration. It is estimated that there were nearly 1 million new immigrants per year by the early 1900s in a country with well under 100 million people. Also, the bulk of these immigrants did not come from northern and western Europe and so were considered decidedly "different." In 1891, Congress required that all immigrants be inspected and that criminals and those with certain diseases be excluded. In 1907, this law was tightened further and extended to entry from Mexico. But the high-water mark of anti-immigration sentiment was the 1924 bill that restricted immigration except from northern and western Europe. President Coolidge signed the bill, saying, "America must remain American." Presumably, that meant northwestern European. But like the Scots Irish of Jackson's day, the wave of immigrants of the 1890–1914 period came into their own politically, tossing out Coolidge's Republicans and becoming a key bloc in the Democrats' New Deal coalition.

Thus, globalization has always been a key American political issue: with the free movement of labor, capital, and goods, an integral part of both our economic development and our political process. By and large, the issues were decided on either a sectional political basis, as in the case of trade, or a political ethnic basis, as in the case of immigration. **In the past, the national interest came second to factional interests within the country. Today, the American political process may arrive at the same result by default, but it is a result that we are less able to afford.**

GLOBALIZATION AND AMERICAN POWER

The American use of foreign capital and immigrant labor historically had an opportunistic component. The Pacific Railway Act that authorized—and subsidized—the first transcontinental rail link was passed at the height of the Civil War. It is doubtful that the actual construction could have been done solely with domestic resources at the same time that much of the native-born male population of the country was engaged in fighting. This symbolic act of national unity at that time was important, but it was also something that could have been deferred.

Today, an end to the process of globalization would not involve merely deferral of national goals. Globalization has been a part of both our national security strategy and our national economic strategy since the end of World War II. **Today, America is not just one beneficiary of the globalization process; it is at the forefront of that process.** At the end of World War II, we used trade as a way of binding together our allies in both the Atlantic and the Pacific. The Bretton Woods Conference established the dollar as the world's key currency. The Marshall Plan provided foreign currency assistance to Europe so that it could afford to buy the goods it needed from America. The International Monetary Fund was set up to minimize the destabilizing effects that swings in trade balances might have. The World Trade Organization (WTO) and its predecessor, the General Agreement on Tariffs and Trade, were set up to establish rules of the game under which foreign trade could flourish.

These were all American initiatives. As a commercial republic, we naturally felt that the prosperity that trade brings would be key both in calming world tensions and in providing an alternative to the extremist ideologies we confronted. And they worked. From the 1959 Kitchen Debate between Nixon and Khrushchev through the collapse of the Berlin Wall and the ultimate decision by China to join the international trading system, the prosperity that our system of economic freedom and trade offers has been one of the banners we hold highest.

This process has transformed both America and our role in the world. When the Smoot Hawley tariff was passed in 1930, our imports were just 4 percent of our gross domestic product (GDP). Today, they are 17 percent. In 1930, the British pound was the world's leading currency, and gold was an integral part of the global financial system. Today, the dollar dominates, and gold is relatively unimportant. In 1950, barely a quarter of the world's population was touched by the global economic system. Today, that figure is nearer two-thirds. Just since 1990, the number of workers involved in countries that are part of this global trading system has more than doubled and is well on its way to tripling. There is no going back, at least not without crippling the global economy and destroying America's leadership role in it.

So the national interest demands that we act to preserve, improve, and hopefully expand the system that we have put in place. That does not mean that the current system is cost free. It does mean that as president, you have a responsibility to sufficiently mitigate those costs that the political process does not revert to a reversal of all that we have gained. There are four areas that require your attention: finance, trade, immigration, and intellectual property. They are the standards for the free flow of capital, goods, labor, and ideas.

INTERNATIONAL FINANCE

The dollar is the world's preeminent currency, and New York City remains the world's financial capital. Both of these facts are recognition of America's leadership role in the global trading system. Both provide huge net benefits to the U.S. economy—but neither one is guaranteed, and preserving them will require some political sacrifices on our part. Some of your predecessors have chosen not to make the required sacrifices, and the costs have been large.

The dollar became the world's reserve currency following the Bretton Woods Conference of 1944. The choice was obvious because there was no other. The dollar was pegged to the old standard—gold—at a fixed rate of $35 per ounce. But the dollar effectively replaced gold because while the amount of gold available is relatively finite and increases at less than 2 percent per year as more is mined, the quantity of dollars is flexible, what economists call "elastic." Thus, having the dollar replace gold allowed the amount of money used to support the world economy to grow much faster, thus facilitating rising levels of well-being and growing world trade.

Other currencies, in turn, were pegged to the dollar at fixed exchange rates that their countries chose. Some, like Britain, chose too high an exchange rate that reduced their competitiveness and made their exports chronically less than their imports. But that meant shipping more money overseas than was being returned. Periodically, Britain ran out of money and was forced to devalue (lower) the value of its currency relative to the dollar to restore supply and demand to balance.

Other countries, particularly Germany and Japan, pegged their currencies at a very low rate relative to the dollar. This made production in their countries quite cheap and led to their rapid industrialization and rising world competitiveness. In turn, they chronically sold more of their goods as exports than they took in as imports. This meant that money flowed into their countries, some of which they put to use in the industrialization process and some of which they accumulated as a reserve. Unlike Britain, they felt no financial pressure to change their currency's value; they weren't running out of money—they were accumulating it. Moreover, they liked the idea of having an undervalued currency, as it made them export powerhouses. Their citizens were made poorer in the process since they were being "underpaid" in world terms, but their political processes tolerated it.

Thus, there was a bias in this fixed exchange rate system. Currencies that were overvalued relative to the dollar (like Britain) had to cut their currency's exchange rate, but countries that were undervalued relative to the dollar (like Germany and Japan) felt no pressure to raise the value of their exchange rate. On net, therefore, most of the world's currencies tended to become undervalued relative to the dollar, or, stated differently, the dollar became overvalued. We developed Britain's problem of losing international competitiveness because of our currency, but, unlike Britain, we didn't have the option of devaluing it—it was fixed by Bretton Woods at $35 to the ounce of gold.

President Johnson's expansionary policies ultimately brought the end to this system. The combination of deficit spending and easy monetary policy led to inflation. With higher inflation, other countries preferred to hold gold rather than dollars. Over time, with the U.S. current account balance deteriorating, financial markets began to bet on a revaluation of the deutschmark in early 1971. Central banks, in particular Germany's Bundesbank, were forced to buy dollars they didn't want to keep their currencies from rising. If they didn't want the dollars, they could ask the United States to convert them for gold.

President Richard Nixon ultimately found the system untenable. Nixon confronted a slowing economy in 1970 as well as a reelection battle in 1972. He felt, probably correctly, that the back-to-back recessions of 1958 and 1960 probably cost him the White House to President John F. Kennedy. He also became a convert to Kennedy's "New Economics," which had included a massive cut in personal and corporate taxes to stimulate the economy, famously saying, "We are all Keynesians now." He pressured Fed Chairman Arthur Burns to stimulate the American economy in the run-up to the election while attempting to curb domestic inflation with wage and price controls. This caused imports to surge further, sending a flood of dollars overseas.

Under Bretton Woods, countries could demand that America redeem excess dollars for gold at $35 an ounce. That exchange rate had been put in place a quarter century before when the world economy was much smaller. It was a ridiculously low price at that time. By demanding gold for dollars, other countries effectively began a "run on the bank." Nixon had no choice but to close the "gold window" and end the Bretton Woods fixed exchange rate system.

What then quickly developed was a "floating" exchange rate system where the value of currencies is set in the market by supply and demand. If a country is exporting too much, it is supplying less of its currency to buy other countries' goods than other countries are demanding to buy its goods, and the price goes up. Under these market-driven rules, the dollar tended to fall at first and the German mark and the Japanese yen tended to rise. Since 1980, we have had a number of episodes in which the dollar has both risen and fallen, and the system, though not perfect, has tended to work fairly well. There are two lessons in this for you as president:

First, **China has been seeking to emulate the Japanese postwar economic miracle by keeping its currency undervalued**. This has led to an enormous surge in Chinese exports relative to imports and has led to the Chinese accumulating more than $1 trillion of reserves, largely in U.S. dollars. We no longer have any legal obligation to redeem those reserves for gold. If they were to demand that we redeem their reserves, we would need simply ask the question a bank teller asks—"Would you like large bills or small?"—and print what is needed. So on a purely financial basis, there is not a lot to worry about. America is getting cheap Chinese goods and paying for them in currency that we have a legal monopoly on printing. You would be in trouble if you did what President Jimmy Carter considered and started issuing U.S. debt in a foreign currency, for then we could not simply print the money. But few of your advisers are likely to recommend emulating Carter's economic policies.

Instead, you have a geopolitical problem and a domestic political problem with this Chinese behavior. By the ethical standards, though perhaps not by the legal standards, of the world trading system of the past thirty-five years, the Chinese are "cheating." They are deliberately undervaluing their currency and rigging their exchange rate in order to gain a competitive advantage for their exports. This is putting

American producers at a disadvantage. It is also putting China's other competitors who play by the rules of the game at a disadvantage. Some of them have already begun copying Chinese policies with regard to fixing their exchange rates. Complicating this is the obvious desire of the Chinese to replace America geopolitically in the western Pacific. To some extent it can be argued that their military development is being financed by their maintenance of an undervalued exchange rate. **Your challenge will be to find a way to manage the geopolitical and domestic political problems of an undervalued Chinese currency without destroying the global trading system**. The techniques you use will depend on how you weight the geopolitical challenge and the trade challenge posed by China.

Second, **you have to take care not to emulate President Nixon and put so much strain on the exchange value of the dollar that it ceases to be the world's preeminent currency**. Like in the early 1970s, the dollar is clearly overvalued on a trade basis. Our imports exceed our exports by a record 6 percent of GDP. This process has been going on since the beginning of the Reagan administration when Paul Volker and Donald Regan allowed the dollar to strengthen dramatically as they battled inflation. Since then, two treasury secretaries explicitly favored a weaker dollar, James Baker under Reagan and Lloyd Bentsen under the Clinton administration, and in both cases the markets obliged, taking the dollar down and causing some collateral damage as a result, including the Mexican tequila crisis of 1994. Nevertheless, the trade deficit has been rising since 1991, in large part because the American economy has been growing much faster than that of our trading partners. As we get richer, we buy more of their goods, while their demand for our goods is held back by their slower growth.

In addition to a change in currency policy by China, there are three ways that our trade deficit can be reduced. First, we could grow much slower. In that case, our demand for all goods, including imports, will drop. Second, the rest of the world could grow much quicker, leading them to increase their demand for our goods. Third, the exchange value of the dollar could drop, leading to a sudden increase in American competitiveness in the global marketplace.

It would be great if the rest of the world, particularly Europe, would grow quicker, but the limit of their sustainable growth is about 2.5 percent, a limit that is still below what is desirable in America. The limit in Japan is about 2 percent, still lower. While China and India have picked up some of this slack, that leaves the choice of much slower growth in America than we have been used to or a sharp drop in the dollar or continuing with very large trade deficits. While a drop in the dollar may seem the best path politically, the potential consequences of such a drop on maintaining the dollar's role in the world financial system are also large. As president, you should take care not to be seen following this path as your preferred alternative.

There is a related question with regard to the preeminence of New York as the world's financial center. Since the passage of the Sarbanes-Oxley Act in 2002 and the flood of separate legal actions by state attorneys general, a good portion of the world's financial activity has moved to London. In fact, when the socialist mayor of London was asked what his economic development strategy for his city was, he replied, "Sarbanes-Oxley."[2]

Thus, our dominance in global financial markets is threatened by our own legal system. The greatest threat is the uncertainty created by fifty separate state laws, each enforced by a politically ambitious state attorney general who sees the opportunity to sue an out-of-state company as a political free lunch. Beyond that is the uncertainty created by a still separate civil litigation process. As president, you should carefully consider legislation to bring more legal certainty to the financial industry. Its effects on America are huge. Fully 17 percent of our GDP in 2006 was derived from financial services, insurance, and real estate, and the profits of financial firms composed almost one-third of total corporate profits. This industry is comprised of both high-paying jobs and a good source of tax revenue and keeps America preeminent in this area as well.

Finally, there is the question of national security and how it affects financial flows. During your predecessor's term, a company in

Dubai, capital of the United Arab Emirates, was blocked from buying a British company with ports in the United States by a political firestorm. No serious apolitical person who has looked at the issue, including both the U.S. bureaucracy charged with assessing the merits and the WTO, felt that the deal's American opponents had a valid case. In fact, just ten years before, the Clinton administration had actively promoted the purchase of the Port of Long Beach by the People's Republic of China. Most people would view China as a bigger long-term security threat to America than the United Arab Emirates. This was clearly unfair, but the world of trade involves a lot of unfairness.

FREE TRADE OF GOODS AND SERVICES

In your campaign, you doubtless found some way of expressing support for free trade that no one could argue with, such as "Trade should be free but fair." For all intents and purposes, America has free trade. The average tariff on our imports is less than 2 percent. Those tariffs we do have are focused on commodities such as agricultural goods. Sugar, for example, has one of the highest effective tariffs (imposed in the form of a quota) of just about any good.

This sugar quota is doubtlessly unfair. But Europe has even higher protection of its agricultural products. Canada has a policy that allows lumber companies to use government land at very low cost. Japan has extensive informal restrictions, requiring, for example, that pharmaceuticals be tested on Japanese and not Caucasians before they can be approved. And these are the relatively "good guys" in the trade arena. Countries like China have extensive formal and informal barriers that favor domestic producers and restrict foreign competition.

The world of global trade is full of unfairness. The question is what to do about it. The standard approach has been to bureaucratize the dispute resolution mechanism, thereby keeping it out of the glare of public and press attention. This helps, but often trade disputes mushroom when the dispute resolution mechanism is exhausted and one party simply refuses to abide by the result. The bureaucratic finding, typically by the WTO, merely allows retaliation against the offending party. But by definition, retaliation takes the form of a low-grade and somewhat controlled trade war. The mechanism is hardly perfect.

Your goal as president should be to depoliticize trade issues as much as possible because when a trade issue gets entangled in domestic politics, it is almost invariably a defeat for free trade. This means appointing a tough, seasoned technocrat with expertise in trade matters to be your trade representative. The more respect he or she has, the fewer disputes will crop up. It will also require you to eschew some quick political wins. **While politics may make it impossible for you to advance the cause of free trade during your administration, maintaining American leadership in the world trading system does require that you not retreat**. That is the minimum standard for what is clearly the national interest.

IMMIGRATION

Politics drives the immigration issue because, as history has shown, a large surge of immigration is often followed by a shift in the political center of gravity in the country. But there is much more to immigration than politics, and both sides in the immigration debate have overstated their case and concern. **As president, you need to be aware of two parts of the immigration question that are neglected in the political debate: economics and bureaucratic management**. While the economic facts of life regarding immigration may not drive your decision, you should at least be aware of the consequences. You should also be aware that so-called immigration reform is a massive bureaucratic undertaking. You might think that you can simply enact reform legislation and leave the bureaucratic nightmare to your successors, but it won't be that simple.

Start with economics. In a market economy, individuals get paid what they are "worth." Economists call this their marginal product—the additional amount of output produced as a result of their participation in the process. While it is true that we do not have a perfectly market-oriented economy, it is a good starting point. So a good first pass on the economics of immigration is that the immigrant will increase the size of our economy but will capture this increase in the wages he or she receives. Other people will be unaffected.

But this is only a starting point. While we have a market economy, we augment the market with a wide variety of government programs and services. Overwhelmingly, these services deliver more money to lower-income people than they collect in taxes. For example, a new thirty-year-old worker earning 45 percent of the average wage and his spouse can be expected to receive, in present value terms, $65,000 more in Social Security benefits than he paid in taxes. The difference between taxes and benefits with regard to Medicare is even larger and larger still if the individual has children. So a higher-wage immigrant will, on balance, pay more in taxes than he or she will get in government benefits, thus lessening the burden on other taxpayers. The reverse is true for lower-skilled and lower-paid workers.

Alternatively, sometimes immigrants are not paid their "marginal product" because of breakdowns in the market economy. For example, Chinese workers who helped build the American railroads in the nineteenth century were paid far less than their Caucasian counterparts. Today, illegal immigrants are often paid less than the comparable pay for their jobs because their illegal status gives them no access to the system to complain. In this case, the exploitation of the immigrants does lead to a net benefit to others—notably employers—but also to the consumers of the goods that illegal immigrants produce.

There may also be large distributional consequences of immigration. An argument has been advanced by immigration supporters that the real wages of current citizens rise as the result of immigration. This may be true on average if the immigrants offer a set of skills not found in the population at large (including a willingness to do jobs natives will not perform) and are sufficiently numerous that they drive down the cost of doing certain functions. Since the goods and services are now cheaper than they otherwise would have been, the incomes of natives are able to buy more of these goods. This argument works best if you assume that the immigrants would not have been producing goods back home that would enter the American marketplace, driving down prices and raising real wages in the process.

This leads to a final economic point regarding immigration: that it can be a way of driving industrial policy. By and large, America has a choice between importing workers to produce goods and services here and importing the goods and services those workers would have produced in their own countries. Consider, for example, the production of lettuce in the Imperial Valley of California. If workers were not imported from Mexico, it is doubtful that the farms of the Imperial Valley would produce lettuce and other crops at a price that is competitive in the marketplace. Instead, those workers could form the basis of an agricultural export business in Mexico that would undercut agricultural production in America. American consumers probably wouldn't even know whether their relatively cheap produce came from Mexico or California. But the landowners and agribusinesses of California would be poorer as a result, and, conversely, the landowners and agribusinesses in Mexico would be more profitable.

The same is true of higher-end products like technology. Many of the companies in Silicon Valley attract skilled technology workers from around the world, most notably from India and China. If our high-technology companies cannot import the workers they feel they need—and you should be aware as president that our laws make this quite difficult—then those same workers will be producing high-technology products in their home countries. We will be importing the technology and goods that they produce instead of importing the workers. Our domestic high-technology industry is then placed at a competitive disadvantage by not being able to get the workers that it needs.

As president, you should be concerned with the industrial policy biases created by our immigration policies and reorient them in a way that favors the kind of industries that you want America to be most competitive in.

But **the biggest immigration challenge that you face regards the bureaucratic reforms that are needed to make our immigration policies work**. At present, we do not really have an immigration policy, unless one thinks that letting anyone who gets here stay virtually unhindered constitutes a policy. There are domestic beneficiaries from this approach. They include the industries employing those workers, typically in agriculture, construction, and low-end manufacturing. They not only gain a competitive advantage from the availability of the labor but also may be able to exploit these workers who lack legal recourse. Other gainers are the politicians and leaders of political blocs who hope to use these immigrants in the present or in the future as voters. The biggest drawbacks to this lack of a policy are a lack of security and a lack of respect for law. After all, when several million individuals enter the country unknown to the authorities, the chances that some of them are undesirable are overwhelming. Moreover, there are millions of individuals both here and around the world who are trying to obey our immigration laws and who are being penalized for doing so.

Simple good governance demands reform, but neither of the two main "reform" camps are advancing ideas that are practical. One camp argues that all those individuals who are now here illegally should have to go home and reapply for entry into America. Of course, no one knows exactly who these people are, as they have escaped detection thus far. Many of these individuals are well integrated into society with families to support and care for, creating a humanitarian challenge, to say the least. Moreover, their sheer numbers—an estimate of around 11 million individuals is commonly cited—suggest that this policy would be a law enforcement nightmare at a minimum and, if successful, would constitute one of the largest forced migrations of people in the history of mankind. This is clearly impractical.

The other "reform" camp talks about "comprehensive" reform that includes a path for citizenship for these 11 million illegal immigrants. One such reform passed the Senate in 2006, but subsequent analysis by nonpartisan Congressional Budget Office staff estimated that its liberal terms would attract an additional 6.5 million individuals by

2016 who would not come here under current law. The impracticality of this approach becomes obvious when one considers what is involved in processing this many people, whether it is the 11 million already here or the more likely figure of 18 million that comprehensive reform would entail.

At present, the U.S. Citizenship and Immigration Services (USCIS) grants around 1 million green cards every year and processes over half a million applications for citizenship per year. No one who has been through the process would argue that this is done in either an efficient manner or a particularly user-friendly one. Moreover, American consulates all around the world now have hundreds of thousands of people in line to apply for green cards. The waiting time in places like Hong Kong for a green card is estimated to be fifteen years. If word gets out that it is now even "easier" to get entry into America, the demand at these consulates would become truly overwhelming.

Imagine that the funds became available to *double* the size of the USCIS staff. None of the "comprehensive" reforms make sufficient room for additional funding—and for good reason. If the financial cost of the program were ever made explicit to the public, support for comprehensive reform would drop still further. Moreover, all existing employees would have to be retrained under the new "comprehensive" law and 25,000 new employees hired. As a practical matter, it would take years to double the size of any bureaucracy in a way that would still allow it to operate with minimal effectiveness.

Doubling the size would allow the USCIS to process the people it would process anyway under existing law plus an equal number of applications from the 18 million who don't currently go anywhere near the USCIS because of their status. At this rate, it would take thirty-six years to clear the queue created by "comprehensive" immigration reform! A minimum of five and as many as nine of your successors will be using your name in vain for the immigration reform legacy you had left them as the swollen bureaucracy consumes resources and the frustrated applicants and their relatives flood you and Congress with complaints about the process.

The politically unmentionable truth about immigration reform is that it is one of those "unsolvable" problems mentioned in a later memo. That is why it is still a problem. But if political pressures now seem inevitable for some kind of reform and you actually want to make it work, here are three points you might consider:

First, any successful reform requires border security first. Just like there is no sense in trying to fill a leaky bucket, there is no sense in trying to normalize the status of people already here if millions more come in illegally every year. This means many more agents than we now have, political and legal support from you as president for the tough job those agents have in carrying out their job, and more physical infrastructure to make the border more difficult to cross. Border security does not just stop at the border, however. Employers and providers of social services must face sanctions if they employ or serve people who are not here legally. If this does not happen, there is no reason for people to jump through the hoops required for legal status.

Second, reform should encourage as many people as possible to "remigrate" back home. The crux of this is the "guest worker" approach to economic integration. Many, if not most, of those now crossing the border illegally come here to earn the higher wages available and remit a portion of their earnings to family back home. They, their families, their country, and our country will all be better off if this process is normalized in a way that also allows them to return home after they have accumulated a nest egg with which to start a more prosperous life back home. Guest workers might, for example, be able to collect their accumulated personal contributions to Social Security on their departure.

Third, employers should be asked to pay for the costs society incurs by admitting the workers they want to hire. The most efficient way of doing this is to charge a fee of, say, $1 per hour or $2,000 per year for all "guest workers" employed. This is also an efficient way of normalizing the status of the 11 million people now here illegally. They can certainly stay in their current employment status and their lives go on as before provided their employer covers this cost. Some might say this is a "tariff" on immigrant workers, and in some sense it is. But unlike goods landing on these shores, these workers are consumers of social services while they are here and are generally quite lightly taxed for the provision of those services. Linking legal status here to employment also ensures a minimum amount of employer-provided security screening.

The greatest advantage to this approach is that it links the bureaucratic challenge of immigration reform with the economic reality of our country's reliance on workers from abroad. These are the two unspoken pieces of the current immigration debate, yet these two pieces also provide the basis for a solution to the problem.

IDEAS

While finance, goods, and people are all important American interests, our real advantage from globalization comes from the free flow of ideas. American culture is one of the most powerful—and subversive—weapons our country possesses. There was a reason why communist dictatorships blocked American radio broadcasts, but there were many items they couldn't block. The American classic board game "Monopoly" was denounced throughout Eastern Europe as a capitalist affectation and suppressed, which, of course, was also one of the reasons why people played it. Today, dictatorships around the world, including many in the Middle East, block American-produced shows from airing on their local television stations. While American game shows, soap operas, and reality television may appear to be politically neutral—if not intellectually vacuous—the culture they show is one that the world envies.

Nor is it just dictatorships that fear American culture; many of our democratic allies do the same. McDonald's, for example, not only is a purveyor of a certain kind of food but has revolutionized the concept of how food is delivered to the public. It is a concept built not just on speed but also on the competitive slogan of a McDonald's competitor: "Have it your way." American fast food upends centuries-old culinary traditions not because it is forced on people but because people like it and particularly like having the choice that it offers.

Hollywood is one of our leading export earners. Cultural elites gather in Cannes to celebrate the "quality" films produced by others, but people worldwide flock to the box office to watch American movies for the masses. Nations like France actually have a quota on the proportion of "foreign" (read American) films that can be shown. Like our cuisine, our movies and our television programming are popular because they are produced not for the elites but for the masses. Indeed, we are one of the few cultures that is truly bottom up in that it is economic demand from below, not artistic sensibilities from above, that determines what is produced.

Another, more political example of this is provided by Fox News. Canada effectively banned Fox News until late 2004. Britain considered a ban on the grounds that "news" is supposed to be objective. One particular objection was that Fox referred to the allied forces in Iraq as "our" troops, indicating that Fox was taking sides, where as "objective" presenters like the British Broadcasting Corporation (BBC) would never do such a thing. The British government overruled complaints about Fox from the BBC and its supporters, perhaps because they concluded that only Americans watch Fox. Yet Al Jazeera played in both Canada and Britain with little protest. The problem in both countries is that Fox, broadcast in English, is not watched only by Americans. (Until the end of 2006, Al Jazeera was broadcast only in Arabic.) It presents a "bottom-up" style of news presentation that both BBC and the Canadian Broadcasting Corporation find competitive.

You may even sympathize at times with those who despise McDonald's, Hollywood tastes in movies, and Fox, but as president you should recognize the powerful symbol that each offers the world of what America is all about. **American culture is attractive because it is anti-elitist in its style while most other countries have cultures dominated by their elites**. One of your jobs as president is to fight for the ability of American culture—and not just our goods exports—to penetrate our trading partners.

But American culture can also be too attractive. One of the flip sides of this is that American culture is also stolen by local producers without a respect for copyright protection. This is as true for higher-end products like Microsoft software as well as for Hollywood films. Yes, we like our culture to be consumed by others, but it is also essential—and even recognized in our Constitution—that patent and copyright protection that assures the inventor a profit is essential to the creation of that culture.

RISK OF A POLICY MISTAKE

We are in one of those times where the pendulum is swinging back on our tolerance of the forces of globalization. You must manage these tensions the best you can, letting off pressure here and there, without making a major policy mistake. America needs massive amounts of global capital to maintain our current pace of consumption and investment. The single biggest mistake of your presidency could be abruptly upsetting these global flows of capital and goods. Such a mistake, if large, could turn a synchronized global expansion into a synchronized global downturn. Tread carefully, Mr. President.

CHAPTER

EIGHT

꧁꧂

TACKLING THE BIG PROBLEMS CONFRONTING AMERICA

A WELL-ESTABLISHED presidential strategy is to make a commitment that something will happen in the distant future, preferably after the president's retirement. Ever since President John F. Kennedy committed the nation in 1961 to putting a man on the moon and returning him safely by the end of the decade—and then was proven right by history with just five months to spare—presidents have been obsessed with moon-shot goals. Never mind that the country lost interest in space just a few years later or that we have never returned to the moon since Apollo ended more than thirty years ago. Moon shots are the things that presidents are remembered for.

It is part of a president's job to rally the nation around a great goal. It provides a unifying mission for the country internally and a sense of national identity to the rest of the world. It is also true that it's hard to achieve a herculean task in a term-limited job. So it would be too cynical to say that this is a mere presidential exercise in promising without accountability. I can't tell you how many times I've been in a White House meeting when some idealistic aide would say, "I'm thinking we really need a moon-shot goal here." And ever since President Kennedy's triumph, we've been inundated with them. We have so many great goals waiting to be accomplished that the nation doesn't know what to rally around.

That suggests that a president should focus on one moon shot at a time. It also means that the goal that is selected should actually be achievable. The country needs to be able to exclaim, "We did it!" Instead, we have a long list of failures or, more appropriately, a long list of things that have yet to be achieved.

Perhaps the best example of overpromising is on energy independence. President Richard Nixon made some of the boldest claims, but he at least had the best excuses. After all, he was president during the lunar landing and had good reason to believe that the nation would accept the charge he gave it. He also was president during the 1973 Arab oil embargo, giving him ample justification. And at that time, independence might have seemed realistic. America had been a net energy exporter as late as 1952, when Nixon was first elected vice president. So he can be forgiven when in November 1973 he said, "Let us set as our national goal, in the spirit of Apollo, with the determination of the Manhattan Project, that by the end of this decade we will have developed the potential to meet our own energy needs without depending on any foreign energy source."

Given that moon-shot goals were still in their infancy, Nixon probably set the deadline a little too early to be believable. President Gerald Ford, a more prudent man, pushed the independence goal back to 1985 and signed into law the Energy Policy and Conservation Act, which established fuel efficiency standards for the first time.

President Jimmy Carter decided to wrap energy policy in ethical terms as a way of inspiring the nation. After only two weeks in office, he appeared on television in a cardigan sweater and asked Americans to turn their thermostats down to a chilly fifty-five degrees. Two months later, he called the quest for energy independence the "moral equivalent of war." Perhaps it was this moral urgency that led Carter to overpromise more than anyone. By 1979, his language had become even more dramatic, calling the energy crisis "a clear and present danger to our nation." In the same speech, he said, "I am tonight setting a clear goal for the energy policy of the United States. Beginning this moment, this nation will never use more foreign oil than we did in 1977—never."[1] Carter's promise was fanciful for a host of reasons but especially so since one of his key policies, a windfall profits tax, directly discouraged new investment in domestic energy sources.

Carter's successor made no such promises on energy independence. President Ronald Reagan was focused on all-out economic growth, and growth would require more energy than our nation could provide on its own. Reagan did away with price controls and import quotas and watched energy prices fall under his two terms, which led to prosperity but also more dependence on foreign sources. He was the most successful, by the measures he laid out, of any president on energy policy. But then again, his goal had nothing to do with energy independence.

President George H. W. Bush and President Bill Clinton made nods toward energy independence, but they were always half-hearted, at least relative to Carter. Gasoline prices dropped sharply relative to wages. Moreover, no nuclear power plants were initiated under either president, cutting off one of the most logical avenues for achieving independence.

President George W. Bush made energy policy a priority in early 2001, only to have it set aside for the most part because of the recession, 9/11, and the Afghanistan and Iraq wars. By 2006, he had reasserted his interest in energy policy by announcing in very modern terms that "America was addicted to oil." Addiction is the modern excuse not for it being our choice but for it being something outside our control. The next year, Bush went on to promise to reduce our use of gasoline by 20 percent in 2017, though he left out of the speech that the goal was relative to an increasing baseline. This shows how presidents have drifted toward creating more nebulous

goals since the early precision of Kennedy. The targets are now far-
ther out in time and the achievements more amorphous.

So if you have no idea what national goal you are supposed to
be rallying behind right now, it's not entirely your fault. Our past
presidents have left you with a lot of orders to fill. That's why I told
our next president to pick just one of the myriad of unsolvable
problems and try to actually solve it. Or, as Norman Vincent Peale
once said, "Promises are like crying babies in a theater: they should
be carried out at once."

MEMORANDUM FOR THE PRESIDENT

FROM: LAWRENCE B. LINDSEY
SUBJECT: UNSOLVABLE PROBLEMS: PICK ONE AND SOLVE IT
January 20, 2009

During the campaign, you addressed a wide variety of issues such as health care, education, and energy. You criticized the current Congress and administration for not doing enough in those areas, and you promised to do more. You won't be the first president to have campaigned on the need to address these issues, and you won't be the last. Large-scale federal involvement in each of these areas goes back at least forty years and includes at least eight presidents.

With all this attention, a fair question to ask is, Why are these problems still around? The usual answer given by politicians who are frustrated is that the "special interests" blocked a solution. At some level that is undoubtedly true, especially if one defines a "special interest" as the 35 million senior citizens of the country or the 160 million workers who pay payroll taxes to cover the costs of Medicare or the 7 million people who work in the country's public schools, or the 70 million parents of school-aged children. Each of these blocs of people has folks in Washington who claim to speak on their behalf, and those organized groups are what are usually meant by the "special interests." These groups have their limitations, but they would not stay in business if they did not faithfully represent a broader class of stakeholders.

But the root cause of unsolvable problems isn't even special interests broadly defined; it is conflicting *national* interests. Politics is always a matter of trade-offs, but sometimes the objectives that must be traded off are quite fundamental. For example, America often struggles to strike a balance between liberty and equality, both of which are deeply seated national principles. We also struggle to find the right balance between the national interest and state and local interests, both of which are enshrined in our Constitution.

Your staff will be recommending that you have to "do something" about each of these problems as well as a variety of other "unsolvable" problems. Politically, doing something means doing something *small* in the sense that what you do doesn't require addressing the larger fundamental trade-off that exists. Small doesn't necessarily mean cheap. In fact, pouring lots of money into a problem is the standard way of finessing the conflicting national objectives and buying off any interest groups that might object. To be fair, each of your predecessors has "done something," just like their staffs recommended. Nearly all were small in effect; some were decidedly not cheap. That is why these problems are still there waiting for you.

You have a fundamental choice between conserving your political capital by doing something small in a variety of areas to make it look like you are addressing problems or actually making a big step toward solving one of these unsolvable problems. Our recommendation is that you do the latter. But you will probably not have enough political capital to do more than one. So, fundamentally, the choice is picking one key problem that you care a lot about and throwing all your energies into it.

This memo considers the root causes of three insoluble issues: education, health care, and energy. But, of course, these are not the only three such insoluble issues. They are presented here as illustrative of the kinds of trade-offs you will face in whatever insoluble issue you decide is worthy of your attention.

EDUCATION: QUALITY, CHOICE, AND UNIFORMITY

The public provision of education became widespread in America during the 1840s. But long before that, America was one of the most literate countries on earth. The parents living in particular towns would often get together and hire a schoolteacher to teach their children the basics. Sometimes churches provided the service. This was particularly easy when a single church dominated a town or a state. As time went on and America became more diverse, competing religious groups set up their own schools. Education happened even without the government involved, but it was far from uniform in either quality or content.

In 1837, Horace Mann became head of education in Massachusetts. Mann believed that state control of education was essential to establishing a common set of values and skills among children. He made sure that textbooks were approved by the state and that the state controlled teachers' colleges, called normal schools at the time.

One of Mann's main concerns—and one that gained many adherents during the nineteenth century—was that the separate school system being established by the rapidly growing Catholic population posed a threat to social cohesion. Uniformity of education was therefore one of the guiding principles of the public school movement from the beginning and an increasingly overarching one. In fact, it became an article of faith among the governing classes.

The principle of uniformity took another step forward after World War II with the move toward consolidation. The number of school districts in the country shrank by more than 85 percent between 1940 and 1990 as larger unified school districts were established. Both local control and local finance were reduced, with the share paid for by local property taxes dropping from more than two-thirds to about one-third over the same period. These measures often went hand in hand with improvements in quality or at least the establishment of some minimum quality standards for all students.

Obviously, the desegregation of public schools under *Brown v. Board of Education* in 1954 was also a step in the same direction. The Supreme Court held that "separate but equal" was *inherently* unequal since the stigma of segregation was an impediment to black children's education. Much of the evidence presented in that case by Thurgood Marshall representing the plaintiffs was statistical in nature and designed to establish that point. The courts followed this logic in the late 1960s and 1970s by enforcing busing programs on schools that were never legally segregated but that had wide racial disparities due to housing patterns.

But uniformity does not always go hand in hand with quality. A one-size-fits-all education program was found deficient as early as the 1950s, as it failed to take account of differences in individual student abilities. Public schools set up "tracking" programs to segment students by their abilities, allowing gifted students to be more challenged and therefore less bored and slower students to learn more at their own pace. Tracking went in and out of vogue with opponents noting that by limiting homogeneity, it was inherently depriving slower students of exposure to their more gifted classmates.

This argument was finessed within the public school environment with the creation of the special education movement and the creation of individual education profiles for students with educational difficulties. Bilingual education programs were set up offering decidedly nonuniform instruction and ethnically segregated classrooms in order to handle the challenges posed by a more diverse student body. But educational statistics do not indicate that any of these efforts has actually resulted in improved educational quality despite the fact that they require significant increases in costs.[2]

At the other extreme, "magnet" schools were created to offer specialized educational programs for students with particular skills or for parents who preferred particular educational programs. These developments were efforts to address a perceived deterioration in quality within the public schools. But they were also evidence of a loss of confidence within the public school system in the general principle that uniformity and quality went hand in hand.

Critics of public schools go further. They argue that all these efforts are proof that Horace Mann's case rested on a desire for control for its own sake, not on an improvement in quality. Uniformity remains in the curriculum but not in the delivery of educational services. In addition, centralization and state control has entrenched one of the few monopolies remaining in the United States, with predictable results. Critics note that all these efforts have not produced any improvement in educational test scores despite the huge increase in costs that has resulted. Inflation adjusted per student spending rose

68 percent from 1980 to 2002 with no discernable quality improvements. Department of Education statistics show that public schools even have higher pupil-to-teacher ratios despite having an average cost per student nearly 60 percent greater than the average tuition of private schools.

Should you choose to address the education issue in a major way, you will have to solve the inherent conflicts between choice, quality, and uniformity—conflicts that date back before Horace Mann's day. For example, you may begin by assuming that parents know what type of education is best for their children. But are you willing to have public funds support schools that contain a strong religious or political bias? In the extreme, for example, should state funds be used to send children to radical Islamic schools that teach that non-Muslims who refuse to convert deserve to be killed? It was this desire to promote social cohesion by teaching a common set of values that led to complete state control of education in the first place.

On the other hand, Mann himself would not argue with the notion that state-controlled education expounds its own religious and political vision. Indeed, that was a core part of his vision. And even in Mann's day, some found parts of this state-approved doctrine objectionable. In fact, it is probably inevitable that many in a free society might find some parts of what the state teaches objectionable. Nor do the statistics support the belief that we now provide a quality of education that is either uniform or high. But stress uniformity, and quality surely suffers both for the most talented students and for the least talented. A related and divisive ethical question is whether good kids should be able to escape bad schools—and the answer often depends on whether the good kid in the bad school is your own.

These are not "special interest" concerns or the kind of "political" concerns that are solved by logrolling. They are fundamental and competing *national* objectives. Layered on top of these fundamental issues, stakeholder issues form another set of obstacles to education reform. The most obvious stakeholders are the teacher unions and the educational establishment itself. They pose an obstacle both to radical reform, as it would destroy the system that is their raison d'être, and to quality improvements within the schools that would enhance accountability.

Before proceeding in this area, you should be aware that our educational system has created another, more subtle set of stakeholders who are numerically even more powerful: middle-class suburbanites. It is an axiom in real estate that good public schools enhance property values and that the search for better-quality schools is one of the motivating reasons behind the rapid growth of America's suburbs in the past half century. Changing the status quo in favor of either uniformity or parental choice destroys that advantage since the *relative* educational advantage offered by living in the suburbs goes away if either schooling magically becomes equal or the school one's children attend is no longer determined solely by where one lives.

A final challenge is that there is a limited amount of reform that can be done at the federal level even if you want, given the high degree of state and local control. Now you know why none of your predecessors have tackled comprehensive education reform. Maybe they were just leaving it for the right person.

HEALTH CARE: RATION BY QUANTITY, BY PRICE, OR NOT AT ALL

Imagine you were tasked with the job of trying to design, from scratch, a way of delivering health care services to the public. Would you require everyone seeking attention—from a routine examination to help for a highly contagious disease—to assemble in one place where they could exchange germs? Would you require the sick to transport themselves to such a place? Would you then require those who require medications—typically, ill and contagious themselves—to transport themselves to yet another venue crowded with healthy shoppers to deliver a handwritten note to someone and then wait an hour so they can shop and mingle some more before picking up their prescription?

Of course, the absurdities of the current system don't stop there. Even with a prescription, terminally ill patients cannot legally get some medicines in America that they could buy without a prescription at any pharmacy in Mexico. The manner of treatment, even down to the number of pills in a prescription, is not determined solely by the doctor after seeing a patient but often by a rule set by an insurance provider who has never even seen the patient. Individuals pay a health insurance provider the overhead costs to process bills that cost less than a tank of gas but would never think of asking an auto insurance company for "gas insurance" or "oil change insurance." If ever a system cried out for change, it is health care.

Still, even with all its warts, we have the best health care system in the world because we don't force uniformity at the expense of quality. Our private-led system adopts innovative techniques faster than government-controlled single-payer systems. This is especially critical given the wave of new technology that is just over the horizon. Soon we will be able to have customized drugs based on our own DNA that will greatly limit complications and adverse reactions. And the benefits of nanotechnology promise much safer ways of doing complicated internal procedures. Health care reform is not just about the present but about the future as well. As in any industry, cost saving today by cutting investment in research will lead to lower quality tomorrow. **One of the most important parts of any health care reform process is to protect the role of innovation, both the creation of new procedures and the earliest possible adoption of these advancements**.

In Washington, of course, reform is usually considered as a monetary issue. This year we will spend over $2 trillion on health care. That is nearly $7,000 per person, $28,000 for a family of four, one dollar in seven of the value of everything our nation produces. But our system costs lives as well as money. An estimated 90,000 people died in 2005 because of diseases—usually infections—that they got by going to the hospital. The Institutes of Medicine estimate that 50,000 to 100,000 people die per year because of medical errors.

Why have your predecessors let this happen?

This system has developed by default, largely as the result of decisions made in other areas. But each of those decisions had unintended consequences for health care. For example, most people have some of their medical costs covered by health insurance that they get through work. That happened as the result of wage and price controls during World War II. Employers seeking to attract workers but prohibited by regulation from raising wages offered health insurance coverage as a "fringe benefit" that didn't fall under the wage and price control guidelines. The idea caught on and spread because of the tax code. If your company were to give you money to buy your own health insurance, both you and the company have to pay payroll taxes on it, and you have to pay income taxes on it. If they give you health insurance directly, no one pays any tax.

Insurance is a good thing, but insurance is fundamentally for protection against unexpected expenses, not for covering routine and predictable costs. The tax code has encouraged first-dollar insurance where we run almost all expenses through a complex and broken system. This means that insurers have to enact cost-savings conditions since neither the doctor nor the patient is sensitive to price. This is at least as true when the government is the insurer as when private companies are. Over time, pressures emerged for the health care delivery system to do things as cheaply as possible.

One early economy was the end of the house call. In fact, you may be among the last people in the Oval Office to know what a house call was. Doctors used to go to where their sick patients were, particularly in the case of children, rather than having the sick patients travel to them. In fact, one of the early magazine advertisements for automobiles portrayed a sick child with the doctor by her side with the banner, "So the Doctor Gets There in Time." Needless to say, the house call system does not economize on the doctor's time—the cost of travel was built into the fee the doctor charged. Insurance companies wouldn't stand for that since the doctor's driving time is not part of what they are insuring; it is a personal service incidental to the delivery of health care. Doctors didn't mind either since it was far easier to move from waiting room to waiting room than from house to house. They could see more patients, make better use of their professional skills, and, presumably, also make more money.

Today, over 80 percent of medical expenses are paid for by "third-party" payers, outside the delivery of the actual service. These payers set rules on what they will pay for each service, rules that in turn changed the nature of health care delivery. One of the best examples was Medicare's willingness to pay for hospital costs and visits to the doctor but not for prescription drugs the doctor might provide. Gradually, this skewed health care delivery away from prescription drugs and toward hospitalization. Evidence mounted that this was driving up total costs of health care delivery since more expensive hospital stays were being substituted for less expensive drugs. The Medicare Prescription Drug Act, passed in 2003, was intended to change this but with the added effect of shifting more of the health care bill onto the government. It was this last part that was the centerpiece of the bill's popularity.

There is a fundamental moral question behind the issue of third-party payer. As a society, we have come to conclude that health care is one of those things in life that people should not be denied because they can't afford it. Today, even people without insurance are still given health care largely through hospital emergency rooms. People there are not turned away because it is unethical (and often illegal) to do so. For the vast majority of the population that does have insurance, the cost of incremental health care is a fraction of its cost, typically twenty cents on the dollar or less. For many, the cost of additional care is zero. **Unlike for most other goods and services in the economy, price is not used to ration health care**.

Whenever a market-clearing price is not used to clear supply and demand for something, two other possibilities develop. One is that the good in question is overconsumed, as people have no financial incentive not to consume. Since someone still has to pay, this means that the total spending by society on that good is far more than it otherwise would be.

The other possibility is that "non-price rationing" occurs. This means that some form of inconvenience is used to stop people from consuming too much. The most typical form of non-price rationing is waiting in long lines. In many countries like Britain and Sweden with government-subsidized medical care, patients are often asked to wait long periods before receiving care. For example, women in Britain may be forced to wait several months to get a repeat mammogram after a first mammogram is abnormal. And more than half the people requiring radiation treatment after cancer surgery have to wait more than four weeks after a doctor ordered it in order to get it, four weeks being the British government's own definition of the "maximum acceptable" waiting time. Those delays are for life-threatening diseases that supposedly are a government priority. So-called elective procedures such as hip replacements are rare. And the reason that the majority of new pharmaceutical patents are received by American companies is that resources are simply not devoted to developing new medicines. Delaying the introduction of new medicine is the definitive way to make people wait on line.

The ultimate choice in health care, therefore, is between increasing the amount of price rationing, increasing the amount of non-price rationing, or continuing to watch a bigger share of both gross domestic product and our national budget go into health care. By and large, your predecessors have tended to choose the third option. It is politically by far the easiest since the costs are diffused among the entire population in the form of higher taxes or larger budget deficits. More important, there are no "poster children" for higher taxes, but there most assuredly are if people are denied medical care either because they can't afford it or because the delays in the system are too long.

There are two intermediate steps that you might want to consider that follow the same logic the insurance companies followed when they refused to pay for house calls, that is, two major costs that are ancillary to the delivery of health care and therefore can be done away with while getting rid of some of the inefficiencies in the system. These changes do involve political costs, however.

The first step is to end the tax subsidization of the third-party payment system, something quite different from ending the tax subsidization of health care. Currently, a worker who pays his or her own medical costs out of pocket receives only a limited tax saving. But the entire cost of employer-provided health *insurance*, including both the medical care costs and the administrative and overhead expenses, is fully tax deductible. This "tax wedge" in favor of third-party payment is typically between 30 and 40 percent for most workers.

There are a variety of ways of doing this. One is provided in another memorandum in this briefing book that discusses tax reform. Another was advanced by your predecessor. It would end the tax deductibility of employer-paid health insurance and substitute a flat $15,000 deduction against both payroll taxes and personal income taxes in its place. Under this proposal, the tax wedge in favor of third-party payment would disappear. Workers with very generous health insurance coverage—more than $15,000 per year—would end up paying higher taxes. Taxpayers with less generous coverage would pay less, and taxpayers who previously had no coverage would receive a major reduction in taxes, enough in fact to defray most of the cost of a catastrophic insurance policy.

There are a number of side benefits to this for both the health care market and the employment market. Health insurance would be less tied to employment and much more available on the individual market. Workers would no longer be tied to their jobs for fear of losing their health insurance, thus creating a more fluid labor market. There would be an incentive to choose plans with higher deductibles and higher copayments. This would reinsert price into the equation, helping to reduce unnecessary spending. Politically, you should recognize that there are a number of employers and labor unions that would not find this to be an advantage, and they will oppose such a reform. But it is an intermediate step toward reform that would not impose either dramatic price or non-price rationing, and, as scored by the Joint Tax Committee, would actually be a major revenue gainer for the federal budget.

The second intermediate step in health care reform has to do with the legal system. The fear of health care related lawsuits has been estimated to increase total medical costs by $100 billion to $200 billion per year. Many doctors leave practice early rather than face crippling insurance premiums and the risk of having a lifetime of practicing medicine destroyed by a single lawsuit. Even more damaging, fear of lawsuits has become one of the major drivers of the delivery of health care. Needless tests are ordered in order to build a file of evidence that "every" step was taken, innovative procedures are not followed, and new medicines are delayed.

The unfortunate truth that we do not like to admit to ourselves is that all medicine involves some risk. This is true of even the simplest medical procedures and of every patented and Food and Drug Administration-approved medicine. We now know that even that oldest and most widely used of medicines—aspirin—has side effects. The right standard cannot be that every medicine and medical procedure has no side effects on anyone in the population, for if that were the standard, there would be no medicine or medical procedures. Punitive lawsuits that assess damages against companies that produce these medicines or doctors who practice the skills they were taught have the consequence of reducing their availability. We have already seen the consequences of this in some states. Some places lost their practitioners of high-risk specialties, such as obstetrics and gynecology, because of the prevalence of lawsuits.

While a case could be made that it is efficient for society to compensate those who have side effects for the economic damages they suffer, it is on net harmful to society for such compensation to go beyond that point. One model worth emulating is offered by the state of California, where the law sets a ceiling of $250,000 on any noneconomic damages that a plaintiff can be awarded.

While these steps offer the opportunity to make the current medical care and payment systems work more efficiently, they are by no means panaceas. Ultimately, the choice comes down to rationing health care services in some fashion or paying the cost of virtually unlimited services that individuals have no incentive to economize on. None of these are attractive options, which is why your predecessors have left this issue on your plate.

ENERGY: ECONOMIC EFFICIENCY, NATIONAL SECURITY, AND THE ENVIRONMENT

The cry went up from all the candidates during your recent election campaign that this country needs an energy policy. Actually, we have one. It's just that it is in bits and pieces. Legislation, lawsuits, and a host of regulatory decisions determine what fuels we use, how much we charge for them, and how they are distributed to their end users. These decisions are ad hoc and set seemingly inconsistent standards, but they do define our nation's energy policy. What we lack is a *coherent* energy policy.

There are three competing goals in energy policy: energy independence for national security purposes, cleaner emissions, and low cost. As with health care, the favored political solution has been to try for all three by avoiding energy taxes and subsidizing alternatives to oil. This favors the traditional path of choosing government spending over tougher choices. But as a result, we have lost ground on energy independence and have been slow to reduce emissions. We have really chosen low cost as the top priority, which is also saying that we have been taking a free trade approach to energy.

Free Trade. Free trade is based on the principle of comparative advantage, whereby each nation should specialize in making the goods and services in which it has a relative advantage. If any place has a comparative advantage for producing oil, it is the Middle East. Not only do they have 57 percent of the world's proven reserves, but their oil is much cheaper to recover than in most other parts of the world. The average cost of recovery for a barrel of oil in Saudi Arabia is $3 compared with a cost of $15 in the Gulf of Mexico. The fundamental reason we import so much oil from the Middle East is that it is cheaper to do so. This access to cheap energy has been a major contributor to the growth of our economy over the long run. Critics will note that instability in the Middle East has and will make crucial oil supplies unavailable at times, causing significant short-term economic pain. These critics also argue that the United States should give greater weight to national security issues in developing an energy policy.

National Security. Even as revered a free market theorist as Adam Smith argued that there were times when the principle of free trade and low tariffs had to give way to concerns about national security. He argued for "some burden" on foreign commerce "when some particular sort of industry is necessary for the defense of the country . . . [since] defense is of much more importance than opulence."[3] So national security—or energy independence as it is often called—is a legitimate question when it comes to energy policy.

Today, we are engaged in a series of massive programs aimed at reducing our dependence on foreign oil. One of the most dramatic is a major reallocation of our corn crop into the production of ethanol. Another is a set of regulatory mandates to improve the gas mileage of our vehicles. Consider how one might apply cost–benefit analysis to the first example.

First, one needs an estimate of how much "energy independence" is worth. As president, your instinct will be to consider it "priceless" because it limits your ability to conduct foreign policy.

Still, neither you nor the country has unlimited resources at your disposal, and you do not have an unlimited ability to do as you please in the foreign policy arena—it is full of limitations. So, while the world is much more than dollars and cents, a financial measure can be a good common denominator for putting things into perspective.

It is probably a good idea to estimate the national security costs of dependence on foreign oil on the high side. To do this, imagine that the entire cost of our military efforts in the Middle East were devoted solely to maintaining access to oil. This is obviously false—we have many foreign policy interests in that region, but for the sake of argument, assume that the line espoused by those anti-American extremists who say that it is "all about oil" is correct. That gives us an estimate of $100 billion per year for our dependence on foreign oil. Each year, America consumes about 7.5 billion barrels of oil, making the per barrel cost of this defense commitment about $13.50 per barrel, which works out to a bit less than thirty-five cents per gallon of gasoline. Now, this may be too low if our military presence ultimately proves ineffective or if our military strategy ultimately causes a confrontation in the Strait of Hormuz that sparks an oil-induced recession. But it does provide a baseline to work with.

Now consider the costs of ethanol as an alternative. At current production levels of 5 billion gallons of alternative fuels, ethanol is only modestly more expensive than gasoline at the wholesale level: $2.29 versus $2.07 as of this writing. However, after accounting for federal tax credits of 51 cents per gallon, the total cost difference is roughly twice the national security premium of 35 cents per gallon. Additionally, your predecessor recommended increasing alternative fuel consumption to 35 billion barrels by 2017, of which about 14 billion barrels was to come from corn. Under U.S. Department of Agriculture estimates, that would require consuming over half and potentially all the corn we now export either directly or in the form of livestock that eat the corn. Bearing in mind that the United States is the largest agricultural exporter on the planet, one can get a sense of how big a commitment this would be. Absent a remarkable technological breakthrough, the cost of diverting this much of the planet's food supply into ethanol would swamp the 35 cent national security premium, showing ethanol to be an inefficient solution on national security grounds. The fact that simple cost–benefit calculations like these contradict politically sacrosanct programs like ethanol is probably the reason why a coherent national energy policy doesn't exist.

The Environment. Our natural environment is one of the blessings of America. We have one of the most beautiful countries on earth with endless variety, something that is well worth preserving.

Protecting the environment, though, is a difficult concept to nail down, especially from an energy perspective. Are we trying to build fewer roads? Emit less carbon? Preserve the Alaskan tundra? All the above? Solving each of these problems will provide a different and highly uncertain cost–benefit analysis. The range of uncertainties is so high that it is nearly impossible to calculate an accurate cost benefit, especially with something like global warming. If you have a highly uncertain event like global warming where the potential damage is far off in the future, the most easily justified policy on economic grounds is to favor technological investments with a high potential return over long time horizons.

But another conclusion to draw from this is that the reason we do not have a coherent national energy policy is that issues like free trade, energy independence, and the environment are not ones that the political process considers in the context of rational trade-offs. Rather, they are fundamental value issues like those that dominate the discussion of health care and education.

There are also big regional differences in who favors what energy policies. Northeasterners tend to favor a gas tax, especially if they take the subway to work. These same people will vehemently oppose a tax on home heating oil. Conversely, a gas tax would disproportionately hurt large, poor states like New Mexico, where low-income people might have long drives to make in pickup trucks.

Even with all these challenges, there are a few solutions that make more sense than others. A carbon tax could be combined with a consumption-oriented tax cut to offset the impact on working-class Americans. Such a plan would incorporate a national security and environmental protection premium on the consumption of energy while allowing the principles of free trade to dictate the supply of energy. Politically, though, a carbon tax is a very tough sell. Most politicians prefer some form of cap and trade system on carbon emissions over a tax. The disadvantage of cap and trade system is that it is more rigid, so the economic costs are higher if the cap is set at the wrong level from a cost–benefit perspective.

Another policy that would be a net improvement over our current energy strategy would be an imported oil tax that would kick in if the price fell below a certain level, like $35 a barrel. Such a plan would be likely to collect zero revenue, but by limiting the downside possibilities, it would provide a positive incentive to increase domestic energy supplies, both oil production and alternative sources of power.

There are two common principles that run through well-thought-out energy plans. The first is that the government doesn't pick winners. With a carbon tax or an imported oil tax, the government is not choosing ethanol, or solar, or wind—it is choosing anything other than foreign oil. Note that this is the opposite of our current discombobulated policy, which subsidizes everything from oil to corn. A second common principle is that the plans don't utilize rigid constraints that could cause great economic harm. Of course, these plans have one more element in common—poor politics, which is why energy is on the unsolvable list in the first place.

CONCLUSION

There is no doubt that the country would benefit from education reform, changes in both the delivery of health care and the means of financing it, and changes in a more coherent policy toward energy. The void to be filled in these areas is not new but reflects the political fact of life that significant change in these areas is a matter of overcoming not only certain vested interests (although these certainly exist) but also a more fundamental set of conflicts on national priorities.

As president, you have a finite amount of political capital. If you devote it to tackling one of these supposedly insoluble issues and you succeed, you will leave your mark on the nation and establish your place in history. But your chances of success are not high. If you decide to proceed, you should forgo the strategy of proposing incremental changes in a wide variety of areas since you will not have the political capital to devote to these and concentrate on doing one "big" thing. It is a worthy mission for the next four years.

CHAPTER NINE

THE REACTION
TO FEAR ITSELF

O NE OF THE joys of being an entrepreneur and starting a new business is to not only enjoy watching
the business grow and succeed but also watch the
people who came on board with you when you started the business do well. After all, their prosperity was in part due to the success of your business.

Three months after starting my current business, The Lindsey
Group, in January 2003, both of the company's only two full-time
employees bought new homes. What amazed me—and made me
quite proud at the time—was that the basis for their getting mortgages was their pay stub from my company. Yes, we were doing
well, far better than most three-month-old businesses. Our cash
flow was positive, and we had good prospects, and we're still in
business and doing well today. But a pay stub from a business that
was just three months old didn't strike me as particularly secure
evidence of an ability to pay back a thirty-year mortgage. Moreover, my employees were putting down just 10 percent on average
of the purchase price of their homes, and the lenders had even
offered them the opportunity to borrow more.

Twenty years earlier, when my wife and I sought to buy our first house, we were offering to put 40 percent down and got rejected from nine banks before finally getting a loan through the intervention of a friend. Moreover, the pay stub that I was showing as proof of income wasn't from a start-up but from an employer that had been around for 350 years—Harvard University.

This may all sound a bit like one of those "When I was a boy, we walked to school in three foot snow drifts" kind of stories. But it was true. It was also one of the reasons that when I was a Federal Reserve governor and was made chairman of the Neighborhood Reinvestment Corporation, I was an advocate of easing the credit standards for first-time home buyers. Never in my wildest dreams did I ever imagine that things would ever get to where they were a few years ago.

That was one of the reasons that our economic consulting efforts were focused on the developing housing bubble quite early. But it is also a reason why it is our new president ought to pay attention to how we got where we are. It also happens to be in his own self-interest.

In the 155 years that economists have tracked the business cycle, only four out of thirty presidents have completely escaped recession: Garfield, Kennedy, Johnson, and Clinton. Two met a fate much worse than leading a nation during a period of economic decline. President James Garfield was shot just four months after taking office while waiting in a Washington rail station. The gunman, a disgruntled lawyer who failed to get a desired appointment, apparently wasn't willing to wait for another chance. John F. Kennedy was shot after only two-and-a-half years in office. The other two got out of office just before recessions were about to start. So the new president's odds aren't very good.

Most of these recessions were a product of either changes in monetary policy or swings in the credit cycle—where loose borrowing standards turn strict. Credit cycles create some of our most vivid pictures of business cycles with bank runs, panics, manias, and speculative bubbles. Fortunately, fluctuations in the growth of gross domestic product have gotten less severe over time. Economic expansions are now longer and the recessions shorter. But as long as fear and greed remains a part of humanity, we are going to have ups and downs.

The president who best understood the human element of the business cycle was Franklin Roosevelt. He expressed this in his first inaugural address on March 4, 1933: "So, first of all, let me assert my firm belief that the only thing we have to fear is fear itself— nameless, unreasoning, unjustified terror which paralyzes needed efforts to convert retreat into advance." While he was in touch with the suffering of the time, Roosevelt did not understand the root economic causes of the Great Depression. In the same speech, he blamed the stubborn, incompetent, and unscrupulous "money changers" who "stand indicted in the court of public opinion, rejected by the hearts and minds of men." He broadly insisted that "there must be an end to speculation with other people's money," he called for a balanced budget by "putting our own national house in order and making income balance outgo," and he relegated trade to the back burner. Said Roosevelt, "Our international trade relations, though vastly important, are in point of time and necessity secondary to the establishment of a sound national economy."

Roosevelt's solutions in that first address would have undoubtedly made the situation worse. The fundamental causes of the Great Depression were a near doubling of tax rates to balance the budget, cutting off trade with massive tariffs, and letting the money supply fall by one-third. All these were directly under the control of the federal government, and his ignorance of these facts extended the Depression as he tinkered with ideas like government-set *minimum* prices under the National Recovery Administration. Still, he can hardly be blamed, as the experts were equally in the dark. It wasn't until 1936 that economists started to come to grips with these problems—and only after a manic professor at Cambridge caused a global sensation.

John Maynard Keynes, like FDR, understood the human element of the Great Depression. He understood this because he himself loved to speculate with his own fortune, and the ups and downs of his fortune were probably what led him to incorporate "animal spirits" into his rigorous economic doctrine, the General Theory of Employment, Money, and Interest. This doctrine established a specific proactive role for government fiscal and monetary policy in alleviating high unemployment.

The roots of the theory go all the way back to the fall of 1905, when Keynes first found himself attracted to money and economics. In a letter to a friend, he wrote, "I find economics increasingly satisfactory, and I think I am rather good at it. I want to manage a railroad or organize a Trust or at least swindle the investing public."[1] Keynes went on to trade commodities, stocks, and currencies and was fairly good at buying on the dips in prices. But, like many, he was fully invested during the market crash of 1929, stating beforehand that "we will not have any more crashes in our time." He was wiped out but started buying aggressively again in 1932 at bargain prices and ultimately died a wealthy man. Given his own flaws and passions, it isn't surprising that he was driven to find flaws in classical economics and to find ways for the government to alleviate the business cycle.

Keynes's contributions to economic practice were gigantic by any measure, but when his ideas were practiced to their fullest under President Lyndon Johnson, they ultimately proved inflationary. Government can reduce the business cycle, and government can exacerbate it, but it ultimately depends on whether the leaders understand the nexus of sentiment and government policy. That is the purpose of the next memo.

MEMORANDUM FOR THE PRESIDENT

FROM: LAWRENCE B. LINDSEY
SUBJECT: WE HAVE NOTHING TO FEAR BUT THE *REACTION TO FEAR ITSELF*
January 20, 2009

You were elected in part by empathizing with those who lost their homes during the housing collapse. Home ownership is part of the American dream, and the political effects of that dream turning, at least temporarily, into a nightmare are profound. Many have been surprised by how sluggish the housing market has been, as if the boom years of the mid-2000s were the norm. A full recovery from a popped property bubble inevitably takes longer than expected. A primary reason is that the political reaction tends to be procyclical, making the size of the bubble bigger and the ultimate downturn worse. **It is well worth your time to understand what caused and prolonged the housing downturn so you can deliver on those promises you made to "restore the American dream of home ownership."**

We have been in, to use a euphemism, a buyer's market in residential real estate. While the statistics vary, this has been the largest sustained decline in nationwide home prices since the 1930s. For students of credit cycles and housing, the past few years have been like watching an inevitable train wreck in slow motion. The political and regulatory leadership was mesmerized by the seemingly endless upward movement in both home ownership and home prices instead of realizing that this was part of a credit cycle that would come to an end. Of course, their predecessors were similarly myopic about the stock market during their tenure, believing that "we have repealed the business cycle."

Being mesmerized by a seemingly endless "up cycle" in economics is an occupational hazard. It is not just true of presidents. There is an old saying on Wall Street that "you shouldn't confuse investment genius with being in the middle of a bull market." One difference is that as president, you have some tools at your disposal to increase the odds that you can turn the housing downturn, or bear market, that you inherited into something better. The place to begin is with some details about how the credit cycle works and how it drove the fifteen-year housing boom and the recent bust.

The recent housing collapse was preceded by the biggest expansion in the availability of credit to purchase homes since the end of World War II. This was the key to the cycle because easier credit means that more people can buy homes. More home buyers mean higher prices. Higher prices mean that fewer people run into financial trouble with their home loans. If their circumstances change and they have to sell their homes, the higher prices mean they make a profit and can pay off their mortgage. With fewer mortgages going bad, lenders feel confident enough to ease credit conditions still further, meaning still more home buyers and still higher prices. Everyone is happy and making money.

At some point in this up cycle, a subtle shift occurs that no one notices at the time. Instead of simply taking the easier credit terms as "icing on the cake," buyers find that they actually need the easier credit terms in order to qualify for mortgages big enough to buy the homes at their new, higher prices. Down payments tend to fall as a fraction of the purchase price because people don't have enough of their own money saved to pay the same percentage of the home's new higher value. No one worries about this because, after all, the house will keep going up in value, thereby quickly generating the equity for the buyer that the down payment was supposed to represent. Ways are also found to lower the initial monthly payment. The most typical way is to tie the borrower's interest rate to a floating rate that moves with market conditions. This takes the so-called risk premium out of a fixed-rate mortgage by shifting the risk of interest rate variability from the lender to the borrower. If this doesn't work, then other, more exotic techniques may be used. Again, no one worries because it may be assumed that the borrower's income will rise over time, allowing the borrower to cover the higher costs; at worst, the house will go up in value, allowing the loan to be repaid.

This is the point at which the up cycle starts sowing the seeds of its own destruction because if, for some reason, house prices do not go up further, then the assumption that justifies these easier credit terms disappears. If this happens, both the borrower and the lender are in big trouble. Moreover, for house prices to keep rising, still more buyers have to be found. But credit terms have already been stretched to get even the current number of buyers onto the market. Just like in the game "musical chairs," at some point the music stops.

The downward part of the credit cycle feeds on itself just like the upward part of the cycle. House prices stop rising. Some people who were counting on rising prices get into trouble and default on their loans. Lenders see that the mortgages they were making were riskier than they thought. They raise their credit standards. This takes potential home buyers out of the market. But with fewer buyers, house prices can fall, putting more people into trouble, driving up defaults, and causing lenders to tighten credit terms still more.

This cyclical behavior has happened over and over again in history. Sometimes it is in real estate, sometimes it is in the stock market, and sometimes it happens with business loans. It is embedded in our economic process because greed and fear are embedded in human psychology. Greed drives the up cycle as people or businesses stretch to buy things they otherwise wouldn't have found prudent to acquire and lenders find ways to make them the loans. Fear drives the down cycle as lenders pull back from extending credit and people and businesses try to unload the investments they have already made, hoping to salvage whatever profit they may have made or avoid further losses.

Walter Bagehot, an editor of the London magazine *The Economist*, famously commented a century and a half ago on the preferred policy reaction to credit cycles like the current one in housing. He said, "lend freely at a penalty rate." By this, he meant that the central bank (our Fed, his Bank of England) should let the credit market correct itself in an unfettered fashion, provide ample liquidity for the market to do so, but charge market participants for the privilege, using the price of money and not heavy-handed regulation as a way of restoring some discipline.

Bagehot's recommendation was a contrarian point of view in the nineteenth century and still is today. The more standard incentive for policymakers in charge is to let markets go to ever-higher extremes without supervision on the way up. That way, those in charge enjoy the popularity of a world in which everyone is making money. Then, when the cycle goes into reverse and things fall apart, they jump in and blame the market participants, sharply tighten regulations, and in the process drive the market down further.

America did this in the stock market bubble of the 1990s, letting all the excesses happen with no regulatory interference on the way up, while our politicians claimed that we were in a new era in which an age of endless affluence was upon us, thanks to their sound policies. Then, when the market crashed, they "rounded up the usual suspects," jailed some, and passed tough new rules so that "it will never happen again." The effect of those new rules was to drive the financial services industry out of New York and overseas to London and, to a lesser extent, to places like Hong Kong and Singapore. True to form, some of the very politicians who brought the new regulatory environment into play complained the loudest about the results.

The same sort of cycle occurred more recently in housing. But with home ownership much more widespread and more integral to both our economy and our social fabric, the implications were more profound this time. To begin, consider how we got where we now are.

THE FIFTEEN-YEAR HOUSING BOOM

The latest mortgage credit cycle began two decades ago in the wake of the collapse of the savings and loan industry and the enactment of two pieces of legislation—Financial Institutions Reform, Recovery and Enforcement Act (FIRREA) in 1989 and the Federal Deposit Insurance Corporation Improvement Act (FDICIA) in 1991—that restructured the industry. The savings and loan industry had provided the financing that led to record-setting home ownership in the decades that followed World War II. But it was built on a business model of short-term borrowing and long-term relending that could not survive the inflation and resulting high interest rates of the 1970s.

After some failed experimentation with patchwork solutions during the 1980s, the whole home financing system was bailed out and redone by the politicians of the day. In the process, they made sure "it would never happen again." Part of that process was making credit terms quite restrictive and directing the bank regulatory agencies to force banks to purge their books of potentially bad credits. Regional real estate collapses resulted in Texas, New England, and California as banks stopped rolling over existing credits and gave new credit only under very stringent terms. Bankers at the time called this the "regulatory reign of terror," and the real estate sector went into steep decline.

After working through this housing correction, the mortgage market eventually stabilized and more normal credit conditions emerged. Financial markets are fabulous innovators at times like these. There were three problems with the savings and loans that both the regulators and the financial markets knew had to be fixed. First, they borrowed short term and lent long term so that when short-term rates went up, they lost money. The solution to this was to increase the number and attractiveness of variable rate mortgages and to find a way to hedge the risks on long-term mortgages. Second, the savings and loans were created to make and hold mortgages on their own books, leaving them particularly vulnerable to swings in the housing industry. The solution was to put mortgage market risk on institutions that were more diversified. Third, the savings and loans tended to operate on a very regional basis, leaving them vulnerable not just to national housing market and interest rate swings but to local conditions as well. The solution was to create a national market that could diversify away from regional risks.

The overall solution was to more fully develop a national securities market for mortgages. New institutions emerged that specialized in originating loans by interacting with borrowers. These institutions then sold the mortgages they made to others who specialized in packaging the loans into loan pools. These pools of loans were often national in scope and therefore diversified. Large investors like pension funds and insurance companies could buy a whole package of loans and spread their risks widely. This process was augmented by actions of Fannie Mae and Freddie Mac, two government-created institutions that markets assumed were backed by the federal government. An implicit government guarantee was thus attached to these bundles of mortgages, further increasing the market for them. The process worked well to vastly increase the money available for making mortgages.

One further problem needed to be addressed. A major underserved market remained in low- and moderate-income areas. "Normal" lending standards required a 20 percent down payment on a home, something that often required an insurmountable sacrifice for low- and moderate-income families to accumulate. In addition, the condition of many of these neighborhoods made it unattractive for individual lenders to underwrite specific mortgages, a challenge that could be solved only by viewing lending in these areas as a "public good" that required participation by all lenders.

The response to this came in 1995 as a new set of regulations under the Community Reinvestment Act (CRA) that effectively amounted to a soft quota on lending in these areas. Regulators also substantially eased a variety of mortgage lending standards, including loan-to-value requirements, in order to increase the size of the potential market. (In the interest of full disclosure and perhaps a bit of a mea culpa, I was one of those instrumental in drafting these regulations.) At first, the process worked reasonably well. A new pool of potential home buyers was empowered with access to credit. Housing demand rose. The families who sold homes to new buyers were able to upgrade. With a generalized rise in home prices and significantly eased mortgage availability, default rates and resulting losses to lenders dropped substantially.

Lenders, buoyed by the success of these loans and the low default rates, reduced lending standards still further. They reasoned that if easier lending standards worked well for a population that had historically been higher risk, surely they must work well for the general population. Of course, to adhere to the CRA's "soft quota," that also meant that lending standards had to be further eased for the underserved population. A hardwired cycle of ever-easier credit was created. By 2006, the median down payment for first-time home buyers was only 2 percent, down from a 20 percent standard down payment fifteen years before. Forty percent of all first-time home buyers in 2005 put zero down or actually took out mortgages that were more than the cost of their homes. The credit cycle had gone from extremely restrictive to extremely accommodative, completing half of what is and always has been a round-trip.

In this last credit cycle, ways were found to save on both principal and interest in order to qualify for a mortgage. First was the development of the "interest-only" loan, in which the entire principal repayment was delayed. Second was the widespread use of variable-rate mortgages, which adjusted with market conditions. To some extent, these variable-rate mortgages are quite prudent. Long-term interest rates on which fixed-rate mortgages are based are typically higher than short-term rates because the lender takes a risk that rates might go up. With a fixed-rate mortgage, the lender carries this risk; with a variable-rate mortgage, the borrower carries the risk. Indeed, no less an authority than Federal Reserve Chairman Alan Greenspan recommended that borrowers take out variable-rate mortgages in order to take advantage of this situation.

As the credit cycle got into its very late stages, even more exotic products were created. One was a negative amortization product where the interest rate was deliberately set below the market rate with the extra interest being rolled into the loan's principal. In a rising house price market, this involved little risk to either borrower or lender. Another version of this was a very low qualifying rate with a drastically higher reset rate and a prepayment penalty attached. The lender essentially recouped the lost interest in the early stages of the loan either through payments made at the higher rate or through the prepayment penalty.

The most important point to make is that none of these innovations is malicious in its intent. The purpose of each was to help the borrower qualify for the mortgage. Increasing access to home ownership had the bipartisan support of Congress and regulatory blessing and was coupled with both political and regulatory pressure. Families who never before had access to home ownership because their income, credit history, or neighborhood made them too risky to meet conventional standards now could attain that portion of the American dream.

Of course, financial market participants were not doing this out of the goodness of their hearts but to make money. But the currently fashionable term "predatory" should be used with care when considering the actual nature of this market. "High risk" is a better phrase. In moderation, these added risks were well worth it. But the self-reinforcing nature of this up cycle camouflaged the actual risks that were being undertaken. Inevitably, the dynamics created by the upward spiral create the conditions for a down cycle.

THE HOUSING DOWN CYCLE

While credit market up cycles have their self-reinforcing trends, so do down cycles. We have seen this already in both the real estate market and the mortgage market. With credit availability made as easy as possible in order to make as many mortgages available as possible, there does come a point when there literally is no one else who conceivably could be a home buyer. With houses bid up to historically high prices, sellers often decide that now is the time to take profits. As in any market, whenever there is an excess of supply over demand, the only way the market can clear is for prices to fall.

But the high level of credit in housing makes the price cutting process more painful. For example, consider what would happen if you borrow money to buy a stock in the stock market using the maximum amount of borrowing allowed—50 percent. On a $100 stock, you put down $50 and borrow $50. If the price drops by 10 percent, to $90, you are forced to sell (it's called a margin call) and pay back what you have borrowed. You end up seeing your initial investment drop by 20 percent, from $50 to the $40 you have left after you sell the stock for $90 and pay back the $50 you borrowed.

Now consider what happens when you buy a house putting only 2 percent down, like the median first-time home buyer in 2006. Let's say it is a $200,000 house and you put down $4,000. If the house goes down in price by 10 percent and you sell it for $180,000, you lose all of your $4,000 down payment, plus you still owe the bank $16,000 at the closing. You have no down payment left to buy another house, and your credit rating is ruined by your $16,000 debt. Essentially, you cannot get a mortgage to buy another house. Your response: don't sell.

Now consider the attitude of the lenders. When house prices were going up, it was easy to give someone a loan with a 2 percent down payment. After all, if home prices rose 10 percent, that 2 percent down payment became as good as a 12 percent down payment in just one year. The chances of the home owner not being able to pay you back with that much of a cushion in the house was very small. But when prices are dropping by 3 percent a year, a 2 percent down payment gets wiped out. Your loan is in the classic position of being "underwater" just a year later.

Over time, this effective tightening of credit has a big effect on prices. People who have moved to a new house before selling their original house face the burden of carrying two mortgages. At some point, they get desperate and decide to cut their asking price for the house. This gives appraisers a "comparable price" for other houses in the neighborhood, but the comparable price is very low relative to the recent past. With prices obviously on a down trend, further caution sets in. Everyone in the same neighborhood now is faced with the need to make huge price concessions in order to move their property.

Prices begin a downward spiral. With relatively few sales and those sales that occur happening at very deflated prices, a sort of contagion begins to affect the values of all houses in the area.

The latest credit cycle was exacerbated by the development of the mortgage-backed securities market. As discussed earlier, this financial development obviated the problems that caused the old savings and loan industry to fail. But it set in place a whole new set of pitfalls. Since the new system relied on a separation of mortgage originators who had some knowledge of both the borrowers and the collateral from those who securitized the mortgages and the actual lenders who bought the securities, there was a complete disconnect between the lender and the borrower. Investors who buy mortgages have no idea who the actual buyer of the home was and have never seen the houses that make up the collateral behind the mortgages they are buying. They are relying on the statistical characteristics provided by those who did make the mortgage: a given loan-to-value ratio, a given set of home-owner characteristics with regard to creditworthiness, and a given maximum percentage of mortgage payment to monthly income. Once prices started going down, the statistical criteria on which the bundle of mortgages was sold no longer matched reality. As word gets around that actual default rates in the bundled pools of mortgages are higher than what the statistical models said they were, buyers of the mortgage pools begin to pull back from the market.

HOW WE COULD HAVE ALL
LIVED HAPPILY EVER AFTER

Long before Walter Bagehot wrote his ideas in *The Economist*, credit cycles like the one we experienced in housing have been part of the economic picture. **They are fundamentally about fear and greed, and we won't repeal credit cycles until we change these very human emotions.** The totalitarian ideologies that developed in the twentieth century thought they could do this, but all they did was substitute the mood swings of the megalomaniac in charge or the internal machinations of the Politburo for the functioning of markets. Today, few would doubt that imperfect as they are, markets are less dangerous.

Bagehot's insight was that fear and greed could also be harnessed to force market participants to clean up the excesses of the credit cycle themselves. Credit cycles become truly dangerous when fear gets so excessive that markets break down completely. When no loans are being made, the price of the underlying assets being bought and sold drops precipitously and even relatively good credits with low risks become insolvent. The solution is to let the market function but to nudge it to gradually reduce the risks in the system. The best way to make market participants do this is to make the cost of the credit that is underpinning the system slightly more expensive while still making it available so that buyers and sellers can make their transactions.

Unfortunately, this became a political issue. Even though politicians in both parties claimed credit for rising home ownership during the up part of the credit cycle and were responsible for passing laws and promoted regulations that helped hardwire the credit cycle, they still cried foul when the cycle entered its down phase. **The politicization of the issue helped hardwire the down cycle just like it had helped hardwire the up cycle**.

Actions by government increased the legal liability of lenders, who contributed to the drying up of lending to poorer households. But the needed market correction had already happened, and government simply drove down subprime lending past a new, reasonable level. The supposedly "inappropriate" loans targeted by politicians were by definition ones that used unconventional terms to help the borrower qualify and subsequently went bad. But now, lenders have been doing their utmost to make sure that they don't make any "bad" loans since they don't want to face the liability for their actions. Trouble is, the only sure way to avoid making "bad" loans has been to make hardly any loans at all. The creative financing that allowed millions of families that never used to be able to qualify for mortgages has all but disappeared. The very people that politicians of both parties claimed they wanted to help achieve the American dream suffered the most.

But the biggest potential damage to the nation's mortgage market was from the state attorneys general and the trial bar. The model is well established that suing and jailing rich people in financial markets is a great way for an attorney general to move on to higher office, and this applies equally to both parties. It is, of course, an even more surefire way for an entrepreneurial attorney to get rich by filing a class-action suit. Even when not successful, the constant threat that some trial lawyer or state attorney general seeking higher office might soon be filing suit to get punitive damages for "innocent" victims who were gambling on their teaser-rate mortgages has sent a chill on the mortgage market. It didn't take much guesswork to figure out that both juries and the media were going to side with the little girl and her doll and not with the ultrawealthy Wall Street tycoon.

REGULATORS WERE BEHIND
THE CURVE AS WELL

The politicians were not the only ones behind the curve in the last housing cycle. The regulators, the purported experts, were also decidedly tardy. While the Federal Reserve has done a fine job of following Bagehot's advice regarding monetary policy, it has not been timely in its actions on the mortgage market. It was not until early March 2007 that the Fed and other banking regulators issued a rule regarding subprime lending with teaser rates with large interest rate hikes built in. No one could argue that subprime mortgages that reset at rates many hundreds of basis points higher than the initial qualifying rate were prudent things to issue. But they didn't suddenly become imprudent in 2007, a year and a half after the housing peak; they were imprudent loans to make in 2004 and 2005, when they were all the rage and the Fed was saying little to nothing. This was a clear case of closing the barn door after the cows had already left.

Because this was a credit market cycle, there was no reasonable change in monetary policy that could fully offset the downward spiral once it starts. The Fed, Congress, and the administration should have made every possible legal assurance to market participants that they would not be subjected to massive and unquantifiable legal risk by "doing the right thing" and participating in the mortgage market. Sad to say, but this is exactly the opposite of the political instincts of Washington and of those of the state capitals as well.

RECOMMENDATION: If you are still reading at this point, Mr. President, I applaud your patience for reading about the credit cycle. **The only solution to moderating these cycles is to make sure that at least part of your economic team is contrarian in nature. And you need to be a contrarian yourself.** In good times, ask what needs to be done to mitigate excesses. In bad times, make sure that you are not making things worse. This is never easy, and in your new job it will be much harder than you can ever imagine.

CHAPTER

TEN

❧

THE END OF THE LINE

I

T WAS APRIL 16, 2007. I was grateful for the fact that the fifteenth had fallen on a Sunday. It gave me the extra day to get those tax forms copied and to the post office. It is not that I am a procrastinator—quite the opposite, at least when it comes to taxes. My wife complains that I do taxes all year long, and to a point she's right. Every quarter, I have to calculate my estimated taxes and mail a check to the Internal Revenue Service (IRS), so I have to keep track of where we stand.

The oddity may be that I actually do my own taxes. It is partly a point of pride. In 1985, my thesis at Harvard won the Outstanding Doctoral Dissertation Award from the National Tax Association. It was on the effect of the income tax on the behavior of taxpayers. To do it, I helped write one of the first computer programs for analyzing tax return data provided by the IRS, translating tax code into Fortran. (Younger readers may have to Google "dead languages" to find Fortran among others such as Latin and Aramaic.) My brain has retained such useless facts as the rather complex formula necessary to compute the effective marginal tax rate under the now defunct maximum tax on personal service income and the difference between the alternative minimum tax and the additional minimum tax. So my basic rule is, if I can't do my own taxes having specialized in taxes, then the tax system is a hopeless mess.

Well, on April 16, 2007, I concluded that the tax system was a hopeless mess. I had, as usual, begun assembling the necessary documentation back on the first weekend in January. By mid-February, I knew what documentation I still needed and proceeded to track it down. We went back and forth with one of our brokers (a large national one) about their reporting of interest income to me. They admitted they got it wrong the first time and probably got it wrong the second time as well, but as they say, it was "good enough for government work," which filling out tax forms definitely is.

Then on April 9, my last piece of documentation was e-mailed to me. It was an eighty-page detailed breakdown on a limited partnership I have a small investment in. The importance of the detail was to actually get my taxes right; its net effect on the bottom line on my tax return was $70. I thought I was home free. But I then discovered that I might have a new form to fill out—Form 8615. Actually, I possibly had to fill out two of them, one for each of my two oldest children. The form puts down on paper the new rules regarding the unearned income of minor children. My children had gotten an inheritance from their grandmother that was a nice amount of money but hardly a princely sum. They were now earning interest on the money, but in the end they didn't owe taxes. Still, it was yet another step in a dizzying process.

So there I was, on April 16, copying my tax forms that I had just completed the day before. Why not use a computerized tax filing program? I tried, but unfortunately my life is apparently too complicated for the programs. In fact, not even the IRS seems to be able to get it right. Two years ago, they disputed my return, claiming that I had deducted too much for my and my wife's IRA. I carefully explained to them the painful truth that I had turned fifty and was allowed an additional $500 IRA contribution. One would think the IRS would know that I am fifty since they have all of my life's history. The American Association of Retired Persons certainly knew, how I don't know, having sent me an invitation to join their fine organization. The IRS also got another set of their own rules wrong, and I politely responded to their request for "more information" by quoting their own instructions back to them that I had downloaded from their website.

So why not use a tax preparation firm? My colleague in writing this book also does his own taxes, having been a certified public accountant earlier in life, along with his Harvard-MBA wife. He is someone who has spent a considerable amount of his career in government service, as I have. Given the extra tax scrutiny that comes with high-level public appointments, he decided to have his wife take their tax return to a large national tax preparer to double-check the numbers. The tax firm informed her that they were overpaying taxes related to household help, a key area of scrutiny. After arguing back and forth, with the clear understanding that the client wished to err on the side of caution on any area of interpretation, the professional tax adviser informed her that "nobody pays those taxes anyway." The firm went on to explicitly advise underpaying the legal amount. Needless to say, they are now back to doing their taxes without "expert" help.

Let me stipulate that most people can use helpful tax software, and for many people there is a "short form" that can be completed in a relatively short period of time. But even these people have to assemble the documentation. Besides, most of our income taxes are paid by people who fill out the same kind of forms I do. Aside from the 1040, there is Schedule A, itemized deductions, which is filled out by 46 million people who paid 82 percent of the income tax. Schedule B is filled out by anyone with more than $1,500 of either interest or dividend income. Schedule C reflects entrepreneurial income, which is where the bulk of my income comes from. This also requires me to do Form SE so that I can pay self-employment tax. This is on top of the monthly taxes my business pays when we file our payroll.

Schedule D is for people with capital gains, a type of income reported by 20 million people who, in turn, pay 55 percent of the total taxes. This is one that has gotten far less straightforward. It used to be that you wrote down the investments you sold, how much you sold them for, how much you bought them for, and the dates of the transactions and then paid taxes on your profits. But now there are complicated rules on disallowing portions of your losses and dividing the profits on what used to be a clear-cut short-term gain or a long-term gain into a hybrid. Truth be told, I have no idea how to figure this out and have to take my broker's word for it. I hope they know what they are doing. At least it is a different firm than the one who got the interest wrong. Then there is Schedule E, called the "Supplemental Schedule," for people who may own rental property or are part of a partnership or subchapter S corporation or who earn royalties. The only two major schedules I am *spared* are Schedule F, which is for farmers, and Schedule EIC, which is for low-income earners.

This is a complicated tax life, but, as I said before, I have a PhD from Harvard that is related to this sort of stuff. Moreover, some of the leading brokerages and tax accounting firms, not to mention the IRS, get it wrong too. So I have finally reached the conclusion that we are *at the end of the line with respect to the current income tax system*. It troubles me to do so; if we actually get a real tax reform, then all the brain cells devoted to knowledge of tax detail that I accumulated during graduate school suddenly become redundant. At my age, I don't know if I can even store some other set of barely relevant facts—like baseball statistics—in the space that is freed up.

But complexity is just the tip of the iceberg. The tax system is more than just a paperwork nightmare. *It is a major impediment to economic growth and to the ability of America to compete in the world*. This should be of enormous import to our new president. So please turn the page and find out the logic I used to persuade the new leader of our country why tax reform must be at the top of the agenda.

FROM: LAWRENCE B. LINDSEY
SUBJECT: THE GROWTH IMPERATIVE AND FISCAL POLICY
January 20, 2009

The year 1776 was an important one for American political economy. Not only was the Declaration of Independence signed, but it was also the year that Adam Smith wrote his classic *An Inquiry into the Nature and Causes of the Wealth of Nations*. Both had to do with both politics and economics, and both laid the groundwork for the then somewhat novel notion that one of the key purposes of government was the economic well-being of the population.

The Declaration echoed John Locke's work the century before declaring that we were endowed with certain unalienable rights, including the pursuit of happiness, what Locke had called "property." It added that it was the purpose of government to help secure those rights. It laid specific complaints against the king that could only be considered economic: that he imposed taxes, cut off our trade, and what today we would call "overregulated" the economy. The last was described as "He has erected a multitude of new offices and sent hither swarms of Officers to harass our people and eat out their substance."[1]

Smith pushed similar views not as a set of complaints but as a set of recommendations. He advocated free trade, though as we have noted elsewhere in this briefing book, he did say that national security can trump commerce. He advocated light regulation but not zero regulation. He noted, "People of the same trade seldom meet together, even for merriment and diversion, but the conversation ends in a conspiracy against the public, or in some contrivance to raise prices. It is impossible indeed to prevent such meetings, by any law which either could be executed, or would be consistent with liberty and justice. But though the law cannot hinder people of the same trade from sometimes assembling together, it ought to do nothing to facilitate such assemblies; much less to render them necessary."[2]

On the central theme of this memorandum, fiscal policy, Smith advocated moderate taxation. Two centuries before Arthur Laffer popularized the notion that high tax rates could be counterproductive, Smith wrote, "High taxes, sometimes by diminishing the consumption of the taxed commodities, and sometimes by encouraging smuggling, frequently afford a smaller revenue to government than what might be drawn from more modest taxes."[3]

But these recommendations all fed into a single idea that departed from the conventional wisdom of the day. Smith believed that the wealth of a nation was the productive power of its economy, not the size of the government's (or the king's) trove of treasure. The idea was revolutionary because it called into question a fundamental premise of the development of the nation-state: the state's position depended on its ability to defend itself and, perhaps, expand. This required an army, which in turn was paid for by the king. So the king's ability to pay for the army was viewed as crucial.

Jean-Baptiste Colbert, the finance minister for Louis XIV, was a leading exponent of an early school of economics known as the mercantilists and much more representative of the conventional wisdom. A century before Smith wrote, Colbert developed a policy apparatus that was the antithesis of Smith's view. Colbert focused on repairing the dismal financial condition of the French state while also suppressing a related series of revolts in France known as The Fronde. (The Fronde is French for "sling," the device used by the mob to break the windows of supporters of the government.) Colbert's efforts to simultaneously calm the mob and restore the king's finances led him to a very political solution. He wrote, "The art of taxation consists in so plucking the goose as to obtain the largest possible amount of feathers with the smallest possible amount of hissing."[4]

Note, though, the focus on both collecting as much revenue as possible and doing so in a way that minimizes the *political* ramifications of doing so but not the economic ramifications. Economic historians note that even though Louis XIV's finances improved during Colbert's time in office, the country itself became increasingly impoverished. Smith's *Wealth of Nations* was in large part a rebuttal to Colbert and his policies. **It was the wealth of the nation, not the wealth of the government, that mattered most.**

This is not to say that the wealth of the government doesn't matter. It does. But Colbert's policies missed the point that the wealthier the nation, the easier it is for the government to collect the revenue it needs. So what matters the most to the long-run health of the government's finances is the ability of the economy to grow. It was not that Colbert wasn't a smart fellow; he clearly was. Rather, the desperation of the moment, with mobs in the streets, did not allow him the time for the French economy to grow its way out of its fiscal problems. Of course, the easiest way to have promoted both French economic growth *and* improved the government's finances would have been to shrink the size of government expenditures. But since Louis XIV was in charge, that definitely would have involved far too much hissing from the goose to succeed. So Colbert increased taxes and their economic burden but in a way that temporarily reduced political tensions. Note that this solution was temporary. Louis XIV's descendant lost his head over the matter.

Today, the link between growth and revenue is deeply etched in our own fiscal situation. For example, individual income tax collections were $1,044 billion in fiscal 2006, up 20 percent in real terms from three years earlier even though real economic growth was just 11 percent. Real corporate income tax collections surged 146 percent over the same period, and total taxes rose 24 percent in inflation-adjusted terms. Over the longer term, the government collects roughly 1.4 percent more tax revenue after adjusting for inflation for every 1 percent growth in the real economy.

The debate between Smith and Colbert has been resolved in the American fiscal system decisively in favor of Smith. **As president, you must recognize that without solid economic growth, all your other fiscal plans will not come to fruition.** It doesn't matter whether these plans include new spending programs or an effort to balance the federal budget. In fact, if you mimic Colbert and try too hard to balance the federal budget solely with higher taxes, the result will not be significantly different than the one he faced.

But in the American context, the issue of economic growth has gone far beyond the Smith–Colbert debate. More than two centuries of economic progress and rising standards of living have become ingrained in the expectations of the American people. In fact, it would not be too much of an exaggeration to say that **economic growth is the sine qua non of American political economy**.

This is quite different from the prevailing ethos in other developed parts of the world, most notably Europe. There, economic stability is the main objective. The European Central Bank has a legislative mandate first and foremost to maintain stable prices. The various nation-states concentrate on a hold-harmless fiscal and regulatory policy that makes sure that individuals who lose their jobs keep most of their previous incomes and standards of living, even if they do not find replacement jobs. Of course, there are also numerous regulations that make it difficult, some would say impossible, to actually fire someone. This is stability at all costs, and it is costly.

It is paid for by maintaining very high tax rates on those who succeed even modestly. For example, a four-person family in America does not now even start to pay income taxes until its income reaches $43,000 and then does so at a marginal tax rate of 15 percent on its income over $43,000. In Germany, that family would pay around $6,000 in income taxes and be paying 26 percent on each additional dollar of income. The highest bracket in France, 40 percent, starts at an income of just $87,000 for a single person, only one-fourth of the $336,500 threshold where the American top bracket of 35 percent starts. In Britain, the top 40 percent income tax rate starts at an income of just $75,000. In Germany, the top tax rate of 44.3 percent starts at just $68,000 of income. On top of this, these countries have payroll taxes similar to the American Social Security tax and a value-added tax that is reflected in the price of goods of roughly 17 percent.

Over time, this has also had its effect on growth. In 1980, French per capita gross domestic product (GDP) was 19 percent below Amer-

ica's. Today, it is 27 percent below. Growth has also meant jobs. Historically, America's unemployment rate was higher than in Europe;
today it is far lower. From 1980 to 2005, America added 42 million
civilian jobs, while France, Germany, Italy, and the United Kingdom
added only 18 million.

**The reason growth is essential in the American context is that
it offers the prospect of opportunity.** Without growth, the distribution of economic well-being becomes a zero-sum game. A country
that doesn't grow reverts back to the Colbert dilemma where the state
can grow richer only by making the populace of the country poorer.
And within the context of that stagnant or shrinking pie, the division
of economic well-being is fought over on a political basis, not on the
basis of opportunity for those who work hard, invest, and take risks.

Consider the term "opportunity" in terms of a group in which a
large percentage is starting at the bottom of the economic ladder:
Hispanics. Between 1995 and 2005, the number of Hispanic households in America rose by 58 percent. A large proportion of this growth
came from immigration, and, as noted in the memorandum to you on
this point, those who come here are overwhelmingly at the bottom
of the economic ladder. Despite this influx at the bottom of the
income distribution, the proportion of Hispanic households with a real
income under $25,000 declined, while the proportion of Hispanic
households earning over $100,000 rose from 5.4 to 8.8 percent over
that ten-year period.

This is a remarkable achievement for the individuals involved
who each became an American success story. It is also a real tribute
to the system that let them do so. The success of American immigrants is a story that is probably unmatched in any other advanced
country today. But the most important point for your policy is that
it couldn't have happened without economic growth. Growth makes
such advances not only mathematically possible but politically possible as well. The political tensions that now exist on the question of
immigration would be significantly greater if the gains of each new
immigrant were coming exclusively at the expense of those already

here. **Growth therefore makes your life as president politically easier as well as fiscally easier.**

THE POLITICAL ECONOMY TRADE-OFF

The problem is that progrowth policies are ones that make economic sense and not necessarily ones that make political sense. This was Colbert's dilemma, and it is also true today, though to a lesser extent. Indeed, both Adam Smith and the Founding Fathers recognized a truth that is sometimes overlooked. **The political process exists to deliver goods that cannot be obtained through the normal channels of the economy.** Thus, there is, at a minimum, a tension between what those who control the political process want *now* and what is good for the economy and the political process *in the long run.* The political process, whether it is a Bourbon autocracy or a representative democracy, is designed to, in Colbert's words, minimize the squawking. The more powerful the government is and the more things are decided in the political process, the more squawking drives results.

One of Smith's observations was that economic self-interest is often channeled into political behavior to obtain what cannot be achieved in the marketplace. In Smith's time, this was often carried out by guilds. These producer groups would use the government to stop competition from emerging by lobbying for laws that would restrict entry into the market and regulate the products being produced. While this was done in the name of "quality," such activities effectively blocked innovation. New ways of producing lower-cost products that may have been perfectly safe and adequate were stopped. As noted above, Smith knew that you couldn't stop people with similar interests from getting together but that government "ought to do nothing to facilitate such assemblies; much less to render them necessary." When government gets too powerful or the law gets too prescriptive, then economic interests naturally find it more profitable to try to influence the political process than to produce better-quality goods and services more cheaply. Today, we call Smith's observation "the capture theory" of regulation.

The Founding Fathers also made this intellectual link between big government and a politically driven but not necessarily economically sensible set of laws. The whole system of checks and balances was designed to make it difficult for government to do anything, a fact you will doubtless find quite frustrating as president. Revenue was particularly hard to raise, as all revenue bills had to originate in the House of Representatives. Not only that, the House was specifically made the only part of government that was elected directly by the people. Senators were elected by legislatures, and presidential electors were also chosen in a manner determined by state legislatures. The Constitution went on to prohibit any taxation of exports and any direct taxation of the people. There was no income tax. Taxes had to be raised by apportioning the bill among the states on the basis of how many representatives they had in Congress, something the states naturally resisted. All that was left were tariffs and excise taxes. The Constitution clearly reflected the notion that economic policies should be established not for the benefit of the government but to enhance the wealth of the nation.

America is fortunate because a substantial portion of the American electorate recognizes that things that may sound good politically are not necessarily in their best interest. This widespread personal identification with progrowth policies is what sustains the virtuous circle of opportunity and growth for which America is famous. While you may be tempted from time to time to go for the politically expedient maneuver, in the long run presidential leadership is crucial to keeping a progrowth agenda alive. It is also necessary to stop those in government from capturing the process and running things in the government's—and their own—interest.

ESSENTIAL AND EFFECTIVE GOVERNMENT SPENDING AND REGULATION

The balance that must be struck is a delicate one since there truly are many goods and services that are necessary that only the market can provide. Markets inherently rely on individual ownership to work. For it to make sense for someone to purchase a car, for example, that person should make sure that others cannot use it—that's why we have locks and keys. Economists call this "excludability." Typically, the market also provides goods that are "rival" in their consumption in that if one person consumes the good, someone else can't. Think about an ice cream cone, for example.

Some goods are neither rival nor excludable. Defense is one. If you have a given amount of defense of a country, everyone in the country benefits from it. You can't exclude some citizens from enjoying the benefits of defense whether they paid for it or not. As president, you will doubtless hear complaints that we can't even exclude noncitizens (like the French) who not only don't pay but also act like hissing geese about our de facto protection of them. Defense is also nonrival. The fact that one person is protected by no means diminishes the protection of another person. When goods are neither excludable nor rival, the market can't provide them because there is no incentive for any one person to step up and buy the good.

There are lots of public goods, and this opens the door to lots of inevitable government activities. Clean air is a public good since no one can be excluded from it and one person's breathing does not affect another person (assuming, of course, that you forget about the exhalation of carbon dioxide). Most streets and roads are also public goods, though limited-access highways like interstates can exclude people with tolls, and when there is too much congestion, being on the road becomes rival as well. There is also merit to the argument that maintaining an economic safety net is a public good, although private charities may provide some of this as well. So even in the world of Adam Smith, there is plenty of need for government.

Your challenge as president is to strike the right balance. **One obvious point is that the people who are employed by the government are not neutral observers of how much government is needed.** President Dwight Eisenhower, in his farewell address, made this point explicit when he warned against a capture of government policy both by the military-industrial complex and by the scientific-technological elite: "The prospect of domination of the nation's scholars by Federal employment, project allocations, and the power of money is ever present and is gravely to be regarded. Yet in holding scientific research and discovery in respect, as we should, we must also be alert to the equal and opposite danger that public policy could itself become the captive of a scientific-technological elite."[5] Of course, in Eisenhower's day, neither the health care bureaucracy nor the other social services coalitions were as developed as they are today.

Your Office of Management and Budget (OMB) is there to make sure that the government is getting value for the money it spends on these services. There is also a part of OMB known as the Office of Information and Regulatory Affairs, whose mission is to perform cost–benefit analysis on the regulations being promulgated by government agencies. But OMB operates at a disadvantage. Most of the permanent bureaucracies go directly to interest groups, to sympathetic members of Congress, and to the media. In turn, OMB often is directly in the line of political fire. Their job is to say "no," and "no" always produces more public hissing than does "yes."

There are three questions that you should ask about any government program. First, is it delivering the good that the nation needs? For example, before welfare reform in the 1990s, the "public good" was often defined as the delivery of cash to the poor. Trouble was, the process kept people poor. In this case, the actual good the nation was looking for was temporary support to help poor people transition to a more normal life. Second, is the good being delivered in as efficient a means as possible? A tremendous amount of progress has been made toward privatizing the provision of goods and services in the past few decades. Even the military now uses a large number of civilian contractors. While this process is far from perfect, it generally represents a step toward efficiency.

The third question is often thought of as the most difficult: would the program pass a cost–benefit test? This is what businesses do all the time. They set up a way of measuring the costs of undertaking a project and the revenue that will flow from it. They also use a "hurdle rate of return" to determine whether the investment will pay for itself over time. Government should do the same. Skeptics argue that you can't measure the benefits of a government service. But consider most pork-barrel programs. Take a bridge costing hundreds of millions of dollars to an island with 500 people on it. The costs are explicit, and the benefits are measurable in terms of "free transportation" for those 500 people. The same is true for health care services. In fact, the government itself uses its own calculations for things like "value of lives saved" and other items that are theoretically "priceless."

The key is that as many items in the government budget as possible should be justified using economic logic and not merely as a sop to political hissing. As president, you will undoubtedly do your own political cost-benefit analysis and conclude that taking on a whole variety of special interests is not a good use of your political capital. That is why the final part of this memorandum does a simple cost-benefit calculation for you. The one single reform that you could undertake that would improve the efficiency of government, remove the maximum amount of burden from the economy, and do the most to promote economic growth is tax reform.

A PROGROWTH TAX POLICY

Today, we have a tax system that only Colbert could love. It is not "designed" in the usual sense of that word but rather reflects decades of responding to various choruses of political hissing. First, there is the natural refrain of "soak the rich." Then there is the push back from various producer groups. In true Colbertian fashion, this hissing is rewarded with credits and deductions that have exceptionally complex targets. After all, lawmakers still need to collect the feathers from the geese, so only the most obstreperous get their breaks. Tax policy has also become a tool of social policy with special credits and deductions that are really an alternative form of government spending but done through the tax code.

Subject the current tax system to the three tests described above for cost-benefit analysis. First, is the tax system delivering what the nation needs? Granted that what the nation needs may be viewed as subjective, but in the case of a tax system, "revenue" seems like the right need. IRS studies suggest that there is a "tax gap" in the form of uncollected taxes of about $420 billion in 2006, fully 18 percent of the revenue that is being collected.[6]

Second, is this revenue being collected as efficiently as possible? The IRS estimated that the compliance costs for the individual income tax in 2001 was between $67 billion and $99 billion, or roughly 6 to 10 percent of total revenues.[7] Compliance costs for the entire federal tax system are estimated to be about $140 billion. But this is only the time, legal, and paperwork part of the cost. There is also the question of the economic inefficiency caused by the tax system. One way to show that it is not efficient is to consider what happened when the tax rates on the current tax system were cut. We have three fairly recent tests of this: the 1963–1964 Kennedy tax cuts, the 1981–1984 Reagan tax cuts, and the 2001–2003 Bush tax cuts.

President John Kennedy's final State of the Union Address argued, "I am convinced that the enactment this year of tax reductions and tax reform overshadows all other domestic problems in this Congress. For we cannot lead for long the cause of peace and freedom if we ever cease to set the pace at home." Kennedy's tax cuts were, in contemporary parlance, skewed to the rich. A taxpayer earning $20,000 got a $600 tax cut, while one earning $500,000 got a $123,000 cut.[8] Congress resisted, but Kennedy's martyrdom helped his successor get the bill through. President Lyndon Johnson reportedly told Finance Committee Chairman Senator Harry Byrd in a meeting in the residence that he wanted this done for Kennedy. Johnson, however, reaped the benefits. Real GDP surged 5.8 percent between 1963 and 1964 and a further 6.4 percent between 1964 and 1965. This came from a net fiscal stimulus of just 0.6 percent of GDP, with a tax cut of 1.8 percent of GDP offset by a 1.2 percent cut in federal spending. Even more impressive, although rates were cut between

17 and 30 percent, tax receipts rose by 2.5 percent, and the federal deficit declined from $4.8 billion to $1.4 billion. Most dramatic of all was the surge in revenue coming from the top of the income distribution. Despite a twenty-one-percentage-point cut in the top rate, taxpayers earning over half a million dollars paid 40 percent more in taxes than they would have under the old regime. In short, under Kennedy, **a reduction in rates produced a positive economic result far out of proportion to what one would expect from a simple economic "stimulus" effect, and the response was greatest where the tax rates were cut the most**.

The Reagan tax cuts are more famous. In 1981, Congress enacted a series of staggered reductions in tax rates along with a set of other tax changes that would have the effect of reducing tax revenue. Like Kennedy's tax cuts, the Reagan tax cuts were attacked as being "skewed to the rich." But the tax system was so onerous that despite this, the reduction in top tax rates caused the share of income taxes paid by the top of the income distribution to rise. The top tenth of 1 percent of all taxpayers saw their share of income tax payments rise from just 7 percent in 1981 to 14 percent in 1986. Indeed, an analysis of the tax data from the period shows that the actual amount of revenue collected from high-income taxpayers was more under the new rates than it would have been had the old tax law stayed in place.[9] Once the tax cuts showed up in people's paychecks in a big way in July 1982, the economy took off. What had been a series of recessions that Reagan's predecessor had termed "economic malaise" turned into a series of high-growth years with real growth averaging over 4.5 percent. **Again, the economic response to the reduction in tax rates was far more than what would have been expected simply in terms of short-term economic stimulus, and the response was the greatest where the tax rates were cut the most**.

We have considered in a separate memo the response of the economy to the tax cuts your predecessor introduced. Those cuts came following the collapse of one of the largest stock market bubbles in history and at a time when America faced a terrorist attack.

They were less dramatic in size and scope than either the Kennedy or the Reagan cuts, but their qualitative effect was still the same. **The economic response was greater than what one would have expected from the size of the economic stimulus, and the response was the greatest at the top of the income distribution.**

These recurring facts constitute a smoking gun with regard to the burden of the income tax. **The facts that reductions in tax rates lead to significant economic gains, well in excess of what one would expect from a simple economic stimulus effect, and that those economic gains are concentrated where tax rates are their highest could be possible only if the tax system were imposing a significant economic burden in the first place.** When that burden is reduced, the economy responds.

The economics profession has a range of estimates for how big this effect is. One of the lower estimates that is broadly accepted and incorporated informally into some of the official revenue-estimating models is that a 10 percent reduction in the share of what a high-income taxpayer is allowed to keep after taxes leads to a 4 percent reduction in the tax base. So, for example, if tax rates are 40 percent, a taxpayer is allowed to keep 60 cents out of every additional dollar he or she earns. If the tax rate is increased to 46 percent, the taxpayer can only keep 54 cents—10 percent less than the 60 cents under the old law. This would lead to a 4 percent reduction in the tax base. (Some estimates I did on the effect of President Reagan's tax cuts put that figure at a 7 percent reduction in the tax base for every 10 percent reduction in what a taxpayer can keep.)

An important point to keep in mind is that the reduction in the tax base often reflects an outright reduction in the level of economic activity. But an increase in tax revenue is simply a *transfer* from the private sector to the government. The country isn't any richer when tax receipts go up; the government is richer, but the people are poorer. This is the old Colbert fallacy that an improvement in the economic position of the government reflects an increase in the wealth of the nation.

Consider how this principle works using the example above. If the economy is worth 100 units and there is a 40 percent tax rate in effect, then the public keeps sixty units and the government collects forty units. If the government raises the tax rate to 46 percent, the economic tax base shrinks by 4 percent to ninety-six units. Government collects 46 percent of a slightly smaller pie—and revenue goes up to forty-four units. This leaves the public with just fifty-two units of taxable output. In other words, by raising tax rates to collect an additional four units of revenue, the government had to make the private sector worse off by up to eight units. Note that we're not even talking about the highest point of the Laffer curve, where government revenue is maximized; government revenue is still going up in this example. But the private sector is made worse off by more than the government is made better off. Unless the government is really desperate for revenue, this is hardly an attractive trade-off.

The inescapable conclusion of this comes about mathematically, not from some ideological bias. **Tax rates should be as low as possible**. Of course, since the government has to raise revenue, the flip side of this is that **the tax base should be as broad as possible**.

This is not currently the case. Rather, America is now in a world not too different from the example presented above. Consider, for example, a proposal now being advanced to eliminate the Social Security earnings cap, thus raising the effective tax rate on high-income earners and entrepreneurs from 38.4 to 48.6 percent. Published IRS data from 2004 show that people making over $100,000 (roughly the level of the cap) earned $1.9 trillion in wages and self-employment income, of which about $800 billion was above the cap. Eliminating the cap would raise about $82 billion in net revenue, assuming no behavioral response. In fact, the tax base would shrink by at least 7 percent, or $133 billion. After this response, total tax collections would rise only $27 billion, with Social Security tax collections rising but personal income taxes declining. In this example, the private sector would be made poorer by $6 for every $1 in net additional revenue collected by the federal government.

Thus, the first reason why tax reform now possesses such a big payoff is that the current tax system is near the point of exhaustion when it comes to producing revenue. Raising taxes "on the rich," a classically popular way of collecting feathers while minimizing the political hissing of the geese, is already a very expensive option in terms of the wealth of the nation. But we are also reaching the point where the political hissing may be coming into line with the need for fundamental tax reform.

YOUR ADMINISTRATION'S IMPENDING FISCAL AND POLITICAL CRISIS

An earlier memo discussed why the political process tends to defer problems. These problems tend to build until there is a crisis that virtually requires some president to confront the problem. Your administration is close to that point on taxes. There are two legislative decisions that have to be made regarding taxes in the next two years, most likely in your first year in office. First, the tax cuts that your predecessor enacted to stimulate the economy in the face of the stock market collapse are set to expire at the end of 2010. Second, the alternative minimum tax is now reaching the point where further deferral of the problem is becoming almost prohibitively costly for the federal budget. The political process will have to either tackle these two issues directly or scrap the tax system in favor of something more sensible.

The Bush Tax Cuts. The 2001 Bush tax cuts were passed under a budget reconciliation rule that automatically ended them ten years later. Thus, unless the law is extended, there will be a huge tax increase that takes effect on January 1, 2011. For example, a family of four with $60,000 in income will see its taxes rise from $2,700 to $4,500. The top tax rate will rise from 35 percent to an effective rate of 40.8 percent. The tax rate on dividends will rise from 15 to 40.8 percent and on capital gains from 15 to 28 percent. Of course, this will be a major shock to the economy, particularly when one considers the behavioral responses described above. These points will not be lost on Congress, which faces an election just two months before the tax cuts are set to expire.

As a practical matter, you will have to propose what to do sometime in early 2009 in order to give Congress time to pass the needed legislation. If you propose an extension of the income tax cuts, the estimated five-year revenue cost will be $1.7 trillion, and you will doubtless be attacked for fiscal recklessness. Or you could propose extending just the so-called middle-class tax cuts and let the top rates and death tax increase. This would reduce the five-year revenue cost to $475 billion and doubtless reduce the number of geese who would be losing their feathers. On the other hand, the vast majority of the behavioral economic response will come from letting the top income tax bracket be increased. Recall that the fiscal trade-off at the top end is a reduction in the well-being of the private sector by $2 to $3 for every additional dollar in tax revenue the government collects. Your third choice is to propose a major overhaul of the tax system.

The Alternative Minimum Tax. An early version of the alternative minimum tax (AMT) was put in place in 1969 as a way of making sure that wealthy people did not escape taxation through the use of various loopholes in the tax law. Like the rest of the tax code at the time, the AMT was not indexed for inflation, meaning that higher inflation led to higher taxes. Presidents Carter, Reagan, and George H. W. Bush all raised the AMT tax during their tenure, but it was President Bill Clinton who took the AMT rate up to 28 percent in 1993, the same as the tax rate that hit the middle to upper middle class under the ordinary income tax. At the same time, he rejected proposals to index the exemption levels in the minimum tax. As inflation pushed people into higher brackets, an ever-increasing number got caught by the AMT. This process was accelerated in 2001 when the Bush tax cuts reduced the middle-class tax rate to 25 percent. The Bush plan made temporary adjustments in the AMT to avoid having additional taxpayers pay the AMT, but over time the revenue cost of these temporary adjustments has mushroomed.

In 2009, the cost of merely extending the temporary adjustments for one year will be $60 billion. The AMT by itself will be collecting $667 billion over the next five years, so abolishing it would be exceptionally costly. The flip side of this point is that a huge number of taxpayers are now forced to fill out both the regular tax form and the AMT form in order to comply with the law. If no adjustments are made, 29 million taxpayers will have to file the AMT in 2009, a number that will grow to 53 million by 2017. Even if you propose incurring the $306 billion of temporary adjustments for your four years in office, there will still be millions of taxpayers filing the AMT when you leave office.

As president, you have three choices: 1) You can let the temporary adjustments stop and have a big increase in tax revenue. But, like the expiration of the Bush tax cuts, this will be a fiscal shock to the economy. 2) You can limit but not eliminate the damage by extending the temporary adjustments for the duration of your presidency. Bear in mind, though, that even this temporizing will cost the equivalent of 7 percent of all the tax revenue collected during your term in office. 3) Or you can propose a thorough overhaul of the tax system.

A BROAD-BASED, LOW-RATE TAX SYSTEM

In recent decades, most countries other than the United States have moved their tax systems away from a reliance on the direct taxation of personal and corporate income and toward an enterprise-based taxation of "value added." The value added by any given enterprise-based tax system is the difference between what it sells its output for and what it pays for the raw materials and machinery used to produce that output. Moreover, when it comes to value-added taxes (VAT), world trade rules allow countries to favor domestic production over imports by taxing imports at the same rate as the domestic VAT and by rebating the VAT on exports.

In 2006, the total value added in the American economy was roughly $13.2 trillion. Of this, about $1.5 trillion were added by two sectors that would be difficult to tax: the federal government itself (since the taxes would simply come back in the form of higher spending) and the housing sector. One should also subtract the capital equipment used to produce this value added, which would amount to another $1.3 trillion. In sum, the taxable value added in the American economy was a bit over $10.4 trillion; $760 billion should be added to this figure if, following standard international practice, we subject imports to VAT and allow a rebate of VAT on exports. This would have left an effective VAT tax base of $11.2 trillion in 2006.

Total federal tax receipts in 2006 were $2.4 trillion, meaning that a pure broad-based VAT could have supplied all the federal government's tax revenue at a 21 percent tax rate. That would mean no personal or corporate tax, no Social Security tax, no inheritance tax, and no federal excise taxes like the ones on gasoline, liquor, tobacco, and similar products. If one left the inheritance and excise taxes in place, the same revenue could be raised at a 20 percent tax rate.

This would be the broadest base and lowest rate of tax that would be achievable. It would minimize the economic distortions caused by the collection of government revenue. Enterprises would simply add up their gross receipts, subtract what they paid for raw materials and machinery, and mail the government a check for 20 percent of the difference. Alternatively, the tax base could be calculated by adding up who the enterprise paid money to—employees in the form of compensation, lenders in the form of interest, and shareholders in the form of dividends—and add to that the increase in the cash position of the company to reflect net receipts that were retained. Nonprofit institutions and state and local governments would simply pay a tax on the compensation portion of their expenses, much as they do now with Social Security taxes.

Some might call this a "consumption" tax. But it might just as well be called a "production" tax with a border adjustment for goods shipped overseas. It could also be called a flat tax since income from all sources—employee compensation, interest, and dividends—would be taxed at the same rate. The only difference would be that rather than having each individual fill out a separate tax return, the revenue would be collected at the enterprise level.

One concern expressed about a VAT is that prices might go up. This would be likely if this were a pure tax increase and a resulting increase in costs for all producers. Instead, it is a shift in taxation from one type of cost—payroll and income taxation—to another type of cost—value-added taxation. The shift is revenue neutral. It is true that in the short run some of actual payment of taxes is shifted from households to their employers, leaving people with more money to spend and firms with higher costs. This shift might cause higher prices, particularly in the short run. But the net effect depends more on the behavior of the Federal Reserve than it does on the switch in tax regimes. If the Fed chooses to increase the money supply faster to accommodate the tax change, prices will rise. If it does not so choose, prices will not increase over the long term.

A potentially more legitimate concern is the distributional shift in taxes this might involve. A flat tax is, by definition, a proportional tax in which all people pay the same rate. Today, higher-income people pay a higher percentage of their income in taxes, and lower-income people receive tax credits that sharply reduce or eliminate their income taxes. As president, you could alter your proposal by adding a "high-end" income tax that would affect only taxpayers with substantial incomes. The resulting revenue could be rebated to taxpayers with the same focus on families with children that the current tax credit system would produce.

For example, consider a 20-20 plan. This would involve a 20 percent VAT and a 20 percent flat tax on all incomes above a given threshold. One possible threshold might be $75,000 for single individuals and $150,000 for married couples. This plan would raise enough revenue to include a $2,000 tax credit for every child under age eighteen. It could also include a credit like the current earned income credit, giving a 20 percent credit on wages up to $10,000, for example. If excise taxes and some form of inheritance tax were retained, this plan would also roughly balance the federal budget.

Consider how this would affect a typical family earning $60,000. At present, that family pays roughly $2,500 in income taxes and $9,200 in payroll taxes, split evenly between the family and their employer. Under this plan, they would not file any returns, but their "production" or "consumption" would face an implied tax of 20 percent, or $12,000, roughly equivalent to their current taxes. If they had children, however, they would be receiving a $2,000 credit for each child, putting them ahead.

The effect on high-end taxpayers would also be roughly neutral. Currently, a very wealthy family pays a 35 percent income tax and pays some other taxes. Under this plan, they would have their "production" subject to a VAT of 20 percent and would have an income tax of 20 percent on that portion of their income that exceeded $150,000. Whether the family came out slightly ahead or slightly behind depended on the extent to which they saved and used the deductions and credits in the current system to reduce their income tax liability.

The precise details of any plan that you propose as president would naturally depend on your preferences and the political realities that you face. But a VAT with a rate of 20 percent, coupled with a high-end flat income tax with an identical rate, could be both revenue and distributionally neutral. Such a tax plan would also solve some of the other problems mentioned in this collection of memoranda. For example, it would get rid of the complexity issue *overnight*. Another example is that the current tax-induced discrimination against individual health insurance would disappear.

One of the biggest likely benefits is that it would address the challenge of international trade. Most other countries in the world use a VAT that applies to imports and rebates money to producers of exports, giving them an apparent trade advantage. Some argue that this is reflected in the exchange rates between currencies and that the imposition of a VAT would simply cause the dollar to rise. This is probably true to some extent. But many of our worst trade problems are with countries that fix their exchange rates to the dollar. A shift to a VAT would therefore help redress the trade distortions since the exchange rate would not change.

In conclusion, if you are going to take one single action to maintain the strength of the American economy and promote growth, it would be a shift to a broad-based, low-rate tax system. Taxation, like health care, education, and energy, is one of those problems that presidents talk about as candidates but tend to wind up leaving to their successors. **With the confluence of economic and political forces now facing you at the start of your first term, tax reform may well be the single issue that you can pick that will ensure your place in history.**

CHAPTER ELEVEN

DON'T STAY TOO LONG

YOU NOW KNOW the advice I passed on to the president on how to organize the administration and on how to think about the policy issues of the day. But there is one piece of advice that remains: how to maximize his or her own sense of personal satisfaction and accomplishment. The president did not go through all that it takes to achieve the office simply to do the right thing or to serve the country. If presidents did not leave office personally proud of what they had accomplished, there would be few volunteers to make the sacrifice, and those who did choose to run would probably not be the kind of people we want to lead.

One of the most striking things to observe about our presidents is what happens to them over the time they serve. They visibly age. They cease to be their own person and increasingly become the character they are playing in the great human saga. This tends to leave them a bit hollow on the inside. Pride and a sense of accomplishment is what fills the void.

I admit to having a strong bias on when it is best to serve the president: as early as possible. That is when they are fresh, when they are more the real human beings that first caught the imagination of the country as a real leader. As time passes, they take on the characteristics of the office and gradually become the mere holder of an office that carries with it great responsibility. Despite their best efforts to appear young and fit, their shoulders sag, their hair turns gray, and their eyes lose their sparkle. It is early in their first term that they see the opportunities that lie before them. As time goes on, that sense of opportunity becomes crowded out by constantly confronting the limitations of office.

This leads me to a recommendation that no politician ever wants to hear. It may be a message that all of us dread: know when your time is up. Senators routinely hold office well into their seventies, some even into their eighties and nineties. They have the option of doing so as long as the voters of their state keep returning them. But it matters far less to the country whether some fraction of a 100-member body is past his prime than whether the commander in chief is.

Following is the advice I gave to the next president that is doubtless the least welcome but may be the most important.

MEMORANDUM FOR THE PRESIDENT

FROM: LAWRENCE B. LINDSEY
SUBJECT: GO OUT ON TOP
January 20, 2009

Four years from today will be a day of reflection. That will be true even if you are being sworn in to your second term, and your duties the next day will be the same as your duties the previous day. How can it not be? Just like New Year's Day is a day to look back on what we would have liked to have changed about the past and resolve to do it differently in the future, the same will be true of Inauguration Day. But the time to start thinking about that day is now, for it will determine whether you look back on a successful four years or years of disappointments.

January 21, 2013, will be far different than some random January 2. The clock will be ticking. At that point, the Constitution gives you only four more years to accomplish everything you set out to do as president. The reality of American politics will give you far less time. It is more like a visit of a terminally ill patient to a doctor who is told that you have so many months at most but maybe not that long. So your mental state of mind on that January day four years from now will be far different from what it is today. You will be confronted with limitations, whereas today you face nothing but opportunities.

There is some real irony in this. Most presidents and their staffs spend a good portion of their first term thinking how their actions will affect their chances for being reelected. They may feel subliminally that in that second term they can do "what they really want" because they will be freed of the political constraint of having to run again. In fact, second terms do not turn out well, and presidents usually find themselves increasingly under siege politically, playing defense constantly, and hoping for that day when they will be able to take the political offense. It is a day that rarely comes.

Our constitutional democracy abhors power that is unaccountable. Yet a lack of accountability is exactly what is so supposedly attractive about that second term. Power freed of the need to seek popular vindication is not something we see much of. All presidents assert that they do not seek power for its own sake but rather power "to do what the country needs." It is not the Constitution that specifically constrains them in this but rather their need to remain popular in order to persuade Congress.

Since the end of World War II, ten sitting presidents have had the opportunity to seek another four years in office. Two, Truman in 1952 and Johnson in 1968, chose not to run again for a full second term, having served one term and part of another. The nearly unanimous consensus among historians is that neither could possibly have been reelected and that it was this fact—and some desire to abandon power and return to private life—that drove their decision. Three others, Ford in 1976, Carter in 1980, and Bush in 1992, chose to seek reelection but were defeated by the voters. Five others sought reelection and won.

Those who made it into a second term did not have exemplary records. Truman was energized by a come-from-behind victory in 1948 but got bogged down in Korea. His administration was besieged by a variety of investigations for corruption and for communist sympathizers. His popularity by the end of his second term was near 20 percent. Eisenhower was easily reelected. In his second term, he suffered a heart attack, two recessions, and a decisive political reversal in the midterm elections of 1958. Democrats retained control of both houses of Congress for the next 22 years after 1958.

President Richard Nixon won all but one state in 1972. Twenty months later, he was out of office in disgrace. History is kinder to President Ronald Reagan's second term than were his contemporaries. But he was derided while in office as out of touch, plagued by scandals ranging from Mike Deaver to Iran-Contra. The 1986 elections were a disaster, and even his vice president offered a change in direction to a "kinder and gentler" America in seeking to succeed him. President Bill Clinton's second term was plagued by his impeachment. He left office with good approval ratings but with a Congress turned over to the opposition for the first time in 40 years and a vice president who blamed his failure to win in 2000 on Clinton's behavior in office. Your predecessor had a terrible midterm election and a second term tainted by scandal and was hugely unpopular because of the involvement in Iraq. **None could claim that their second term was better than their first**.

What is interesting about this list is that we do not have a case of a president since World War II who had an excellent chance of being reelected but chose not to run, seeking instead to go out "at the top." There are two cases of a president having done so in the twentieth century. President Calvin Coolidge could have sought reelection in 1928 but chose not to. He is generally considered by historians as having been a bit of an "odd duck," in large part because his personal view was one that did not favor the use of presidential power. So it makes sense that he didn't hanker for another term. He is probably wise not to have done so. His successor, President Herbert Hoover, did believe in active presidential leadership but suffered through the Great Depression and has had his name besmirched as a consequence for ineptitude. Probably it was Coolidge who got the last laugh.

The other example is President Teddy Roosevelt, who had promised the electorate in 1904 that he would not seek another full term, having succeeded President William McKinley after his assassination in September 1901 and having therefore had almost a full term beforehand. Roosevelt went out on a high note and virtually handpicked his successor. But he couldn't stay away from the job. He ran against William Howard Taft in 1912, split the Republicans, and let the Democrats under Woodrow Wilson come back in. In 1917, he tried to revive his image again as a Roughrider by offering to serve in World War I but was quite appropriately ridiculed as a has-been. He, too, probably would have had a better reputation in the long run had he not sought his comeback.

Seeking popular vindication seems to be a common thread in nearly all your predecessors, and maybe our democracy depends on this character trait in all who seek high office. But this record of second terms hardly makes it seem like the reward for having done a good job in the first term is very fitting. Or, possibly, the actual psychic reward comes on election night, and the second term is the price a president pays for the elation of winning.

Whatever the case may be, a president who seeks only "to do the right thing" for the country might be well advised to seek an alternative metric than being reelected to a second term. On average, the country does not do particularly better in second terms than in first terms, and the president himself does decidedly worse. What is particularly unjustifiable is acting in ways during a first term with the sole motivation of being reelected to a second one, as this means doing something other than just doing what is best for the country.

This leads to the recommendation that you begin your first term with the mind-set that you are not going to seek a second term. That way, you will have to focus solely on accomplishing those things that motivated you to run in the first place. You can always change your mind and decide to run for reelection sometime in your third year in office. But starting off with the mental mind-set of being a one termer carries little downside since deferring things to second terms seems to have such a poor track record. And it may actually give you a more successful first term, thus giving you either a better record to run on should it be electoral vindication that you seek, a better place in history, or simply the satisfaction of having done as good a job as you could have. However you cut it, four years from today, on January 20, 2013, you will be happier with your legacy if you act today and each day that follows as if you will be turning over the reins to someone else at that time.

Of course, this does not mean that you have to declare yourself to be in for only four years at the beginning. Indeed, it would probably be foolish to do so. Much of the power of the presidency within his party and with Congress is the implied threat that one may have to deal with him for a full eight years. Once someone is viewed as a short termer—the actual phrase being "lame duck"—then the usual dynamic of political deal making goes away. There is far less incentive to make a deal with someone who will be gone soon and thus unable to deliver on favors in the near future than someone who will be sticking around. That is one reason that second terms do not turn out so well, particularly the last half of the second term.

In fact, there is probably no reason to declare your intentions until late in your third year of office, just after the Congress goes home in the fall of 2011. Everyone will be assuming that you will be running for reelection during 2011 because that is what all your predecessors have done. Even the two who did not choose to run because they knew they would be defeated did not say so until the next spring. So your secret will be safe, and your legislative power will be undiminished in your third year. Since very little is usually accomplished in a fourth year, with everyone focused on the upcoming presidential and congressional elections, almost all of your ability to get things done legislatively will be done by the fall of 2011 anyway.

There is a second reason to make your declaration late in 2011: it will allow you to pick your successor. Assuming that you have been even moderately successful, many of the top tier of candidates in the other party will largely have decided to sit this one out. The odds of a president seeking reelection actually being reelected are high, six in nine. The model of presidential voting designed by Professor Ray Fair at Yale University gives an incumbent seeking reelection a nearly seven-point automatic advantage.[1] That is enough to dissuade the opposition.

It is also enough to dissuade everyone in your own party from running. Taking on an incumbent president of one's own party is not for the faint of heart or for anyone with a sense of history. No one has done it successfully, although by trying some have managed to ensure the defeat of their party's nominee. Patrick Buchanan tried it against President George H. W. Bush in 1992, got almost a third of the vote in New Hampshire, but wound up merely negotiating for when he could speak at the convention. The most successful case was Ronald Reagan's effort against President Gerald Ford in 1976, but it also failed. Eugene McCarthy's near win in New Hampshire in 1968 did help convince President Lyndon Johnson not to run, but it was Johnson's vice president, not McCarthy, who was the ultimate nominee.

A decision by you late in your third year not to run will therefore create a vacuum in your own party and a weakened field in the other party, a natural place for a favored successor. By the way, deciding to run for a second term and winning creates almost the opposite dynamic: it virtually ensures that the other party will pick your successor. Since 1950, only once has a party been given a third term in office, when Bush was elected in 1988. So if succession is the question, your choice is largely between someone of your choosing after one term or of the other party's choosing after two terms.

Three years from now, you may feel that there are good reasons to seek another term. One may be a perceived need to defend your legacy. This was certainly part of the motivation of your immediate predecessor, who found that his decision to invade Iraq was under attack. Doubtless he would have run anyway, but Iraq became the central issue of the 2004 campaign. Similarly, President Clinton must have felt the need to run in 1996 to prove himself after the defeat his party suffered in 1994. But neither could ultimately claim that his second term was better than his first.

Another caution to recall is that popular vindication at the polls or the musings of the chattering class on your tenure in office will involve a whole host of issues. Some of them will have nothing to do with the health and well-being of the country. The mood of the day is determined largely by what the Founding Fathers called "light and transient causes." They cautioned that prudence dictates that these are not reasons to change a government. Your departure from office does not constitute a change in government. The Constitution endures. The institution of the presidency remains. Preserving, protecting, and defending those institutions was all you were constitutionally charged with when you took the oath of office. Your place in history will similarly not depend on the light and transient causes of the moment.

There are only really three questions that you need ask yourself to determine your legacy. 1) Is the country at least as secure today as it was four years ago? 2) Were our essential liberties preserved? 3) Is the nation's economy and social fabric at least as strong as when you took office? Historians will tend to judge you well if you pass these three tests even if your contemporaries did not or even if you were defeated for reelection.

Consider the cases of two of your predecessors for which this is particularly true: Gerald Ford and Harry Truman. During his tenure, Ford was often the subject of ridicule. The press considered him clumsy. His decision to pardon Richard Nixon was deeply unpopular, and his inability to convince Congress to continue aid to the South Vietnamese regime caused the collapse of that government and scenes of an ignominious American departure by helicopter from the roof of our embassy in Saigon.

Yet by the time of his death thirty years after he was defeated, there was nearly universal respect for the decisions that he made. His pardoning of Nixon was considered to have been essential for healing the wounds after what he had called "our long national nightmare" of Watergate. He had inherited an economy in deep trouble but left office with both unemployment and inflation on their way down. Moreover, his alleged "clumsiness" was counter to the reality of a very athletic man who skied well into his eighties and who lived longer than any other president in our history. The nation remained secure and our liberties intact, and Ford's unassuming and down-to-earth nature remains a model to be emulated.

History has had over half a century to evaluate Harry Truman, and few presidents have seen their stock rise more dramatically since the time they left office. Truman certainly had a troubled presidency. Corruption scandals ran into the cabinet level and into senior aides at the White House. At one point, 166 Treasury Department officials had to resign en masse. Over 20,000 government employees were investigated over questions of loyalty and communist affiliations with nearly 3,000 of these either resigning or being fired. The war in Korea was a lodestone around Truman's neck. A Roper poll reports that at one point he had a lower approval rating than any other president before or since.

Yet his decision to resist the expansion of Soviet communism with the Marshall Plan and the formation of the North Atlantic Treaty Organization, and other alliances is widely respected today for having laid the basis for our ultimately successful Cold War strategy. The economy remained troubled, but he began the process of establishing racial equality by desegregating the armed forces by executive decree. All these actions were extremely courageous politically. The left wing of his party deserted his reelection effort over his anticommunist foreign policy with former Vice President Henry Wallace running against him on the Progressive Party line. The segregationist wing of his party also deserted him over his desegregation efforts rallying around Senator Strom Thurmond of South Carolina. Unpopular at the time, these actions have stood the test of history. Truman laid the basis for postwar security and began a process that ultimately strengthened America's social fabric.

At the other extreme, landslide reelections are no indication of historic approval. Both Johnson and Nixon won 61 percent of the vote. Johnson carried forty-four states, Nixon won forty-nine. Both left office in disgrace. Nor has history been particularly kind, despite each having had some successes. Johnson will always be viewed favorably for his efforts on behalf of civil rights. But much of his programmatic approach in the Great Society is today widely regarded as ill conceived. His prosecution of the Vietnam War was ineffectual and largely incompetent. His administration was also riddled by scandal, and his economic policy is credited with having begun the process of inflation. The widespread rioting of 1968 stands as clear evidence that Johnson did not leave the social fabric stronger.

Nixon also had his successes, particularly in opening relations with China. But like Johnson, his landslide reelection has been followed by a dismal historical evaluation. Both Nixon and his first vice president were forced from office by corruption. His economic policies are widely viewed as failures, made worse by the apparent effort to incur long-term costs for short-term help in his reelection bid. Few would judge the nation more secure as the result of either of these presidents. Both whittled away at fundamental liberties by using the government to spy on their domestic enemies. Neither could be viewed historically as having strengthened either our economy or our social fabric.

This brings us back to the point where the first memo in this collection began. You, like your predecessors, will be sorely tempted by the way those around you treat you to forget the reasons why the public put its faith in you. Your ability to stay true to yourself and not confuse your title "president" with your identity—when everyone refers to you as president as if it were your first or last name—is crucial. You are not the office that you inhabit, and the office is not you. This will be the key reflection as you board Air Force One on January 20, 2013, or January 20, 2017, for what will be your last flight.

That flight will be back to a place that you used to call "home." There is doubtless truth to the idea that no one can ever truly go home again. But that is certainly true of ex-presidents. You will forever have the reminders of your office around you. The title is for life. The security is ever present, if somewhat less intrusive. The watchful eye of history will keep its focus, and the historical commentary will only intensify.

Regardless how these four years will have gone, you are owed the gratitude of the nation. But I now have one favor to ask. Breaking in to the Oval Office to leave you these memoranda was not an easy task. It is probably not one I could pull off again. Besides, you will have actually served in the office, while I was merely an observer. I would encourage you to leave a set of memos for your predecessor, either these or your own. He or she deserves to know some of the things you have learned these past few years because I am sure that one of your most wry reflections will be that your successor has no idea how much his or her life is about to change.

NOTES

CHAPTER 3

1. Bob Davis, "Bush Economic Aide Says the Cost of Iraq War May Top $100 Billion," *Wall Street Journal*, September 16, 2002.
2. Davis, "Bush Economic Aide Says the Cost of Iraq War May Top $100 Billion."
3. http://www.jerrypournelle.com/archives2/archives2mail/mail408.html #Iron.
4. Seymour Hersh, *The Dark Side of Camelot* (Little, Brown, 1997), 64.
5. Hugo Black, *Korematsu v. United States*, December 18, 1944.
6. John M. Barry, *The Great Influenza: The Epic Story of the Deadliest Plague in History* (Viking, 2004), 123.
7. Barry, *The Great Influenza*, 125.
8. Barry, *The Great Influenza*, 122.

CHAPTER 4

1. Kenneth Thompson, "John F. Kennedy and Revisionism," *Virginia Quarterly Review*, Summer 1994.
2. Thompson, "John F. Kennedy and Revisionism."
3. Thompson, "John F. Kennedy and Revisionism."
4. Michael Dobbs, "Inside the Mind of Osama Bin Laden Strategy Mixes Long Preparation, Powerful Message Aimed at Dispossessed," *Washington Post*, September 20, 2001.
5. Scott Simon, "An 'Unsettling' Holocaust Debate in Iran," National Public Radio, December 16, 2006.
6. Andrew Roberts, *A History of the English Speaking Peoples since 1900* (Weidenfeld & Nicolson, 2006).

7. John Maynard Keynes, *The Economic Consequences of the Peace* (Harcourt, Brace, and Howe, 1919).

CHAPTER 6

1. Federal Reserve Board, "Federal Open Market Committee Meeting Transcripts," http://www.federalreserve.gov/FOMC/transcripts/1996/19960924Meeting.pdf.
2. Federal Reserve Board, "Federal Open Market Committee Meeting Transcripts."
3. The Federal Reserve Board, "Federal Open Market Committee Meeting Transcripts."
4. Lawrence B. Lindsey, *Economic Puppetmasters: Lessons from the Halls of Power* (AEI Press, 1998).
5. In "The Macroeconomic Effects of Tax Changes: Estimates Based on a New Measure of Fiscal Shocks," March 2007, Professors Paul and Christina Romer estimate that an exogenous tax increase of 1 percent of GDP reduces GDP by 3 percent after ten quarters. In its January 2007 baseline, the Congressional Budget Office (CBO) estimated that the cost of extending the two Bush tax cuts would be $254 billion in fiscal year 2012 (budgetary effects of selected policy alternatives not included in CBO's baseline), a year in which it estimated that GDP will be $17.2 trillion. Thus, not extending the tax cuts would be equivalent to a tax increase of 1.5 percent of GDP. Applying the Romers' elasticity of 300 percent to the 1.5 percent of GDP tax increase results in an estimate that not extending the tax cuts would reduce the level of GDP by 4.5 percent.

CHAPTER 7

1. James Markusen, Melvin James, William Kaempfer, and Keith Maskus, *International Trade Theory and Evidence* (McGraw-Hill, 1995), 343.
2. Michael Harrison, "London Beware: NY Is Wising Up," *The Independent*, December 1, 2006.

CHAPTER 8

1. Jimmy Carter, "The President's Proposed Energy Policy," April 18, 1977. *Vital Speeches of the Day*, Vol. XXXXIII, No. 14, May 1, 1977, 418–20.

2. For instance, the National Assessment of Education Progress shows little if any improvement in national reading and math scores from 1971 to 1999. There is some evidence of improvement in younger children from 1999 to 2004 that may be attributed in part to the No Child Left Behind Act of 2001.

3. Irwin Stelzer, "Hugging Russian Bear May Lead to a Mauling for EU," *Sunday Times,* January 14, 2007.

CHAPTER 9

1. Murray N. Rothbard, *Keynes, the Man* (Ludwig von Mises Institute, 2003).

CHAPTER 10

1. http://www.archives.gov/national-archives-experience/charters/declaration_transcript.html.

2. Adam Smith, *An Inquiry into the Nature and Causes of the Wealth of Nations,* 1776.

3. Smith, *An Inquiry into the Nature and Causes of the Wealth of Nations,* Book 5, 1776.

4. *Bartleby.com* Classic Quotations.

5. Dwight D. Eisenhower, "Farewell Address," January 17, 1961.

6. "New IRS Study Provides Preliminary Tax Gap Estimate," Internal Revenue Service press release, March 29, 2005.

7. Eric J. Toder, Internal Revenue Service, "Estimating the Compliance Cost of the U.S. Individual Income Tax," 2003, 19.

8. *Newsweek,* January 14, 1963, 18.

9. Lawrence B. Lindsey, *The Growth Experiment: How the New Tax Policy Is Transforming the U.S. Economy* (Basic Books, 1991), 83.

CHAPTER 11

1. Ray C. Fair, "The Effect of Economic Events on Votes for President: 2004 Update," November 1, 2006.

ACKNOWLEDGMENTS

WE WOULD like to thank first and foremost our wives, Susan Lindsey and Cassandra Hanley, for tolerating our frequent encroachments on family time while writing and editing the book. We would also like to thank everyone at Rowman & Littlefield for accepting this project on short deadline and specifically acknowledge Jed Lyons for his enthusiasm for the project and our editor Christopher Anzalone for his thoughtful suggestions. We would like to pay special gratitude to the talented Andrew Sacher for his keen eye in checking our facts and figures and for the long hours he devoted to the project. Finally, we would like to thank Karolin Junnila and Elizabeth Koustmer for reading early drafts and helping to keep us on deadline.

INDEX

ABOUT THE AUTHORS

LAWRENCE B. LINDSEY was assistant to the president for economic policy and director of the National Economic Council at the White House (2001–2002). From 1997 to 2001, he was a resident scholar and holder of the Arthur F. Burns Chair in Economics at the American Enterprise Institute. During late 1999 and throughout 2000, he served as then-Governor George W. Bush's chief economic adviser for his presidential campaign. Lindsey served as a member of the Board of Governors of the Federal Reserve System (1991–1997). He was a special assistant to the president for policy development (1989–1991). He was an assistant then an associate professor of economics at Harvard University (1984–1989). From 1981 to 1984, he served on the staff of the Council of Economic Advisers, ending as the senior staff economist for tax policy. He earned his A.B. magna cum laude from Bowdoin College and his M.A. and Ph.D. from Harvard University. He was awarded the Outstanding Doctoral Dissertation Award by the National Tax Association. He is the author of *The Growth Experiment: How the New Tax Policy Is Transforming the U.S. Economy* (Basic Books, 1990) and *Economic Puppetmasters: Lessons from the Halls of Power* (AEI Press, 1999). He is currently the president and chief executive officer of The Lindsey Group, a global economic advisory firm, which he cofounded in 2003.

MARC SUMERLIN is managing director and cofounder of The Lindsey Group. He previously served as deputy assistant to the president for economic policy and deputy director of the National

Economic Council for President George W. Bush. Prior to the White House, Sumerlin was economic policy adviser at the Bush–Cheney 2000 campaign headquarters. He has also worked as a senior analyst and assistant economist to the U.S. Senate Budget Committee. He holds an M.A. in applied economics from Johns Hopkins University and a Master of Public Policy from Duke University, where he was a Senator Jacob Javits Fellow. He graduated magna cum laude and Beta Gamma Sigma from Georgetown University with a B.S. in business administration. He is a term member at the Council on Foreign Relations.